Stepping Into The Sunshine

A MEMOIR OF RECOVERY, LOSS, LOVE AND LAUGHTER

JEAN SWALES

For Shirley and Little Bill.

CONTENTS

PROLOGUE 1

CHAPTER ONE 3

CHAPTER TWO..12

CHAPTER THREE 16

CHAPTER FOUR 23

CHAPTER FIVE 30

CHAPTER SIX 35

CHAPTER SEVEN..41

CHAPTER EIGHT 45

CHAPTER NINE..55

CHAPTER TEN 61

CHAPTER ELEVEN 70

CHAPTER TWELVE..78

CHAPTER THIRTEEN..86

CHAPTER FOURTEEN 100

CHAPTER FIFTEEN..109

CHAPTER SIXTEEN 117

CHAPTER SEVENTEEN..124

CHAPTER EIGHTEEN..127

CHAPTER NINETEEN..134

CHAPTER TWENTY 144

CHAPTER TWENTY-ONE..148

ABOUT THE AUTHOR 153

ACKNOWLEDGMENTS

I give profound thanks to Marnie Summerfield Smith from Your Memoir for her expertise, patience, and encouragement, especially at times when remembering became painful. This memoir, of which I am now very proud, would never have been written without her experience in memoir writing.

I would also like to thank my daughters Julie, Kate and Sarah who have all supported me in their individual ways. It was Julie who actually found Marnie for me.

I thank my granddaughter Ellen for helping me choose photos and send them to Marnie and my son-in-law Jonathan for his technical assistance.

I also thank my dear friend Sally Gregory who has unfailingly shown interest and encouragement in this project of mine.

Also Dyfed Edwards who designed such an appropriate cover for Stepping Into The Sunshine.

PROLOGUE

In the last book I wrote, Blossom and Me, I travelled around England in my campervan interviewing grandmothers and granddaughters about their lives. I was fascinated by how interesting and varied their stories were, so when I got home, I thought I would write a little about my life.

When Blossom and I began our journey, I was quite lost. It had been four years since my husband, Rick, had died. In the early stages of my grief, I didn't even want to leave the house, so to go off on such an adventure, solo, was a considerable undertaking. I knew that it would be a time of great reflection for me.

I was a grandmother by then, but two of my grandchildren lived abroad, so I hadn't spent much time with them. What amazed me on my journey was how so many women of my generation had lived through extreme poverty and how differently their granddaughters were living. The women of my generation suffered not just crippling financial insecurity but were also thwarted by poverty of opportunity. One lady came from a family who were tremendously poor. They did have a small television on which she would watch University Challenge. She knew the answers to every single question. And what was she encouraged to do with her intelligence? Nothing.

What I also witnessed was that the granddaughters were very open about their feelings. The grandmothers didn't know they had feelings! They were stoic about everything. And they were sticklers for discipline – the girls said their grandmothers were strict.

My background was not one of financial poverty, but I could certainly relate to many women whose lives and hearts were full of unacknowledged feelings. Mine is a story of going from living unconsciously to consciously – a story of understanding what had happened in my family and what had happened to me.

But for the first part of my life, I had no idea. It would be half a century before I was forced to see what the hell was going on.

This book is for all women who are stepping into the sunshine or would like to take the first steps towards doing so. I say to you all, be brave. Many of us are walking this path. It's beautiful out here, and you and your whole selves are welcome.

CHAPTER ONE

Like many of the grandmothers and granddaughters I spoke to on my trip with Blossom, the times we live in now are unrecognisable from the time I was born in 1932 at my maternal grandparents' home, Park Lodge in Brockley South, London.

1932 was the year that Women's Own magazine – with concerns about women's rights – was first published. Women may have had the vote by then, but there was no shift in male superiority and power. My mother, Constance Johnson, was born in 1908 and before she married, I believe she played at secretarial work. She wanted to be a nurse, but her parents wouldn't allow it. She was a reluctant housewife and the last thing she wanted to do was run a house. My father, Donald Marriott, was born the year before my mother. He worked for his family company as a lighterman, a highly-skilled worker who operated a lighter – a type of flat-bottomed barge.

Constance and Donald were children of the Edwardian era when parents believed you could spoil a child by giving them too much affection. Hugging was rare and firm discipline was thought to be best. Their parents were brought up in the Victorian era when, for middle-class families like mine, there was even less affection for children.

Not surprisingly then, discipline was very important to my family. Politeness, manners, best behaviour – it was all expected. On one occasion, when I was staying with my mother's sister, Aunt Kath, I didn't finish my lunch. That particular day we were supposed to be having tea with her mother. I adored my grandma and loved visiting her as she always made me feel special. I had dressed with great care in preparation.

At lunchtime, when I stopped eating before my plate was empty, Aunt Kath told me, "If you don't finish your food, you're not going to have tea with grandma." I continued to refuse to eat so she picked up the telephone to call my grandmother.

"Mother," she began, "I'm afraid we won't be…"

But she didn't get any further because I started to gobble up my food. This might seem like a small thing, and of course children must be encouraged to eat, but there was no consideration of the fact that I may have been full up, or too excited to eat. I was angry at Aunt Kath for issuing this threat and scared knowing that she really meant it.

On another occasion, my sister Shirley, who I called Shirl, didn't eat her tea, so Aunt Kath served it to her for breakfast the next morning. Even today, I don't finish what's on my plate as a small act of rebellion against being told that I must eat whatever I had been served.

"Hold your knife properly."

"Hold your fork properly."

These were the other rules. In addition, we were given three smacks on the arm for a lie and five on the bottom for disobedience. I don't remember that happening very much but when it did, I felt embarrassed naturally, but also numb and resigned to what was happening.

As children, we did occasionally fib and disobey but not excessively. My mother smacked my brother William, known as Bill, once and then sobbed her heart out. It was just all so ridiculous because she adored her son, but he had told a lie, so it had to be beaten out of him.

Aunt Kath told me that that Grandma Johnson had a stick in a drawer in the dresser in the kitchen. It was never used but Aunt Kath and my mother knew it was there. One day my mother and her sister broke the stick and threw it, but the next day it was replaced. Discipline was based on fear. It influenced everything.

We were never asked what we liked. We were told

what we liked. I always had the second nicest bedroom at home but that meant if anyone stayed, I was put in a very small room. No discussion, it was just done – life felt very unsafe.

* * *

The first house I remember was in Catford, also in south London. When I was two and a half, my sister Shirley was born, and one of my early memories is of her is of her climbing out of her cot. As she grew older, our days were filled with school and play. Shirl and I loved our garden, playing hopscotch, hide and seek and enjoying our dollies in their prams. There were family holidays every year when a house was rented on the southeast coast for a month. My father came down for a week or two. My maternal grandparents also rented somewhere nearby and friends of my parents and family members came to stay. We went to the beach in all weathers and when we were all there together, playing beach games, we looked like a gypsy encampment.

Before we left home, my mother would put a card in the window of our house. It had the letters CP on it, very large. This was so Carter Patterson, the luggage firm, could collect our suitcases and take them to our destination. My mother would be weeks washing and ironing for the holiday. By the time we went away there were very few clothes we could wear as they were, "already packed." I believe my father took us to where we were staying, although we may have travelled by train.

On Saturdays, my parents took Shirl and I to Blackheath Wanderers Cricket Club – still in existence today – where my father played cricket. My mother helped with the teas and Shirl and I played with the other children. I had piano lessons and studied ballet too. I even danced in a show at Catford Town Hall in 1939. I was nervous and once I'd peeked through the curtain and saw the audience, I didn't want to go on stage. My mother bribed me by saying she would take me to go and see Snow White and The Seven Dwarfs at the cinema. It worked and off we later went to see Disney's latest masterpiece. But so much for a treat – I didn't sleep for weeks afterwards. That witch haunted me!

I know that I was lucky to have such treats as holidays and dance classes. The family timber business did very well.

And there was undoubtedly joy in our home. My parents laughed and joked. They played tennis and bridge and entertained a lot. The extended family were very involved in our lives, everyone lived nearby. My maternal grandparents and sometimes Aunt Kath and her husband, Uncle John, came for Sunday lunch, which my mother cooked. It was a typical lunch and while my mother was a wonderful cook who made great celebrations cakes for family and friends, she was extremely messy. She told me once that she sprinkled flour on the floor to get herself in the mood. She'd make this frightful mess then swan off and leave everyone else to clear the kitchen. When she iced cakes, every doorknob in the house would be sticky for weeks!

But in addition to these amusing memories, meals at home when it was just my immediate family, were quite scary. The atmosphere was tight with the demands of my mother's discipline. On one occasion, my father winked at us children to try and break the tension. We all exploded with laughter, but not happy laughter, the nervous kind. My mother would hit our knuckles with a knife if we weren't holding our cutlery properly. I was rude to my mother once and my father slapped me across the face and made my nose bleed. It did bleed easily in those days, and I was especially pleased it bled on that occasion.

My dear mother had a very cutting tongue and could silence me with excruciating suddenness by correcting my speech or manners. She had a dreaded expression, "One must bow to convention." My sister and I were sent to elocution classes because my father considered that the way we laughed wasn't ladylike enough. My father probably thought the way we laughed was fine, but someone probably mentioned it and that was that. We only went once. We had to laugh in a scale of musical notes, and we couldn't do it without falling about laughing.

When I was very young, I developed a stutter, which I think was due to a continuous fear of not, "getting it right". I was an amazing young girl and I deserved more. We were repressed and inhibited. Is it any wonder I couldn't get my words out?

I always say they broke the mould when they made my mother. She was full of contradictions. Her moods fluctuated from happy to sad and between organized to disorganized. This chaotic nature of hers was represented perfectly by the way she drove. She had never had to take a driving test, and I don't know where she learned to drive. She was a terrible driver, and everybody used to moan about it, although they continued to ask for lifts. Other drivers continuously shouted at her, but she took no notice. Fortunately, there weren't many cars on the road, which eliminated some of the danger. After my father died, she bought herself a Hillman Minx convertible. On one occasion, she raced through a green light from quite a distance. "I made it!" She shouted. Everything was a game to her when she was in the car. One the flip side, she did once go to court for crossing a yellow line but managed to prove that it was in the wrong place. Vindication!

People used to say, "She's a great character, your mother," and I would reply, "Yes she was a great character, but she wasn't much fun to have as a mother." This is true. She wasn't tactile with us children – of course she was likely just as much a product of her upbringing as we were. But the way she was gave me the sense that I was invisible.

We had a maid, Bertha, and she made the beds, did the ironing, the washing up and cleaned the kitchen after my mother had been in there. She never hugged us. She was just there, which was very important to me, but I wouldn't go as far as to say that I loved her or felt loved by her.

We had to be in our bedrooms by 6pm, which was the time my father got home. So even if we were upstairs playing for two or three hours before we went to sleep, we had to be upstairs. I have a memory of laying in bed listening to the old lawn mower – as my father attended to the grass – such a lovely sound. Everything was all right when I heard that sound. I feel the same when I hear it now, although of course the modern mower doesn't make the same nostalgic hum.

But it's my memories of Friday nights at Inchmery Road that stand out as truly and wonderfully happy. That was the night my father would bring home chocolate bars. I looked forward to his arrival with a Cadbury's Crunchie and a Cadbury's Flake – a favourite to this day – no wonder I lost all my teeth. I don't know if he brought some for my Mum, but he'd bring this chocolate upstairs to me. I can't remember if I ate it in bed, but I do recall that I was about six, maybe seven, and he would then scratch my back as I went to sleep, which was just gorgeous. It was very unusual for a parent, especially a father to be so tactile in those days but I loved this close and natural contact. I absolutely adored my father and understand now that I had him on an unrealistic pedestal all my life. He hadn't a clue how to be a father, in all honesty. Not at all. But he knew how and when to deliver chocolate.

CHAPTER TWO

My father's grandfather William Marriott formed the family business of William Marriott & Sons Lighterman and Watermen in 1858. It grew rapidly during the international heyday of the London Docks.

His son, my grandfather – also called William – became an apprentice to his father and later became a Bermondsey City Councillor and chairman of the Rotherhithe Conservative Party. He played bowls for England against South Africa.

William married Ethel, a waitress. I don't know where William and Ethel met or anything about their home life, but they married in September 1905 in Deptford, going on to have my father and his younger brother, Bill. Tragedy struck when Ethel, pregnant with her third child, fell from a stool while putting up curtains and died of a haemorrhage. The baby was also lost. I only learned this about Ethel in recent years and hope that I have an opportunity to visit her grave. Due to her untimely death, I don't know much about my father's mother, but I was given to understand that she was a very pretty lady and apparently Shirl looked very like her.

After Ethel died, my grandfather remarried a woman called Maida. She and my grandfather kept my father at home but farmed poor Bill out to live with a spinster aunt. The boys missed each other terribly. I don't think Maida was a very warm person, so I assume my Dad didn't get much attention from her. That and the loss of his own mother affected him deeply. He could never totally manage to be consistently warm and loving. Uncle Bill spent the rest of his life trying to find love in all the wrong places.

William and Maida Marriott went on to have Doug, born in 1918, Maida, born in 1921 and Malcolm, born in 1923. Bill, Don and Malcolm kept the family business going until 1970, ending an era of at least 11 continuous Marriott lightermen on the River Thames.

My maternal grandmother, also called Ethel, was the younger sister of William Marriott. There had been a lot of inter-marrying between the Marriott and Johnson families in the late 1800s as they all worked on the River Thames. She and I went on to have a close relationship.

* * *

I hardly knew my mother's father Grandpa Johnson. But there was something sinister about him. When she was in her 90s, Aunt Kath told me that he was not a nice man. She had always spoken highly of him, so I was surprised at this late admission. I do know that he was a gambler and in his later years, a drinker.

It's said of my maternal grandmother Ethel, that after she had two children, my mother and Aunt Kath, there was no more sex, which is why my grandfather turned to drink and gambling. Or maybe there was no more sex because he was a drinker and a gambler.

About 15 years ago I was shown a video by my cousin Pam of him at my Aunt Kath's wedding to Uncle John, where I was a bridesmaid. Grandpa Johnson was kissing Aunt Kath as she got in the wedding car, right on the lips. Very proprietorial. Something quite horrid about it, predatory. I told Pam that I never wanted to see that video again.

Grandpa Arthur did the same to me and my cousins, kissing us on the lips and pressing very hard as he did so. They have also said how unpleasant he was. I knew he had crossed a line and I hated it, although I couldn't have told you why at the time. Shirl was also kissed by him. I saw it, but she and I never discussed it. I suppose that even though we didn't like it, we just thought it was normal.

Nobody would have listened if I had said I didn't like it or believed me if I said it felt wrong. I knew that. The behaviour of her father certainly wasn't something I considered discussing with my mother.

My heart knew it wasn't okay.

But at that time, I didn't know how to give my heart a voice.

CHAPTER THREE

"Lord, keep us safe this night.
Secure from all our fears.
May angels guard us while we sleep
Till morning light appears."
A nightly prayer said by my mother, Shirl and me.

When, in 1939 I turned seven and the Second World War began, the docks in London continued to operate, which meant my father didn't have to fight. But my mother, Shirl, and our baby brother Bill – who was just a few months old – and I needed to be evacuated. Since my paternal grandparents had bought a house in Worthing, West Sussex, that was where we went.

The specific dates and places of my evacuation and the schools I attended throughout my childhood are hazy in my mind. Probably because by the time I had finished my education, I had attended between 10 and 12 schools. We stayed in Worthing for a while though, and Shirl and I attended Kingsdene School as weekly boarders for a while.

Quite a while later, my mother got a job at an army convalescent home in Donhead St Mary, in Wiltshire. She was the housekeeper and was able to take Bill to stay with her there. Shirl and I were sent to a boarding school in Shaftesbury, and we hated it; Shirl was only five and cried every night. We pushed our beds together so we could hold hands, but we were separated by a beast of a woman – Janet Brewis. You could say that it's odd that I don't always remember exactly where I was but that I recall that woman's name. But you wouldn't forget somebody who tried to separate you from your only relative. Shirl and I ran away. We walked down Shaftesbury High Street holding hands, wondering why people were staring at us. Then it dawned on us that we had nowhere to go, so we went back to school.

We returned home to Bromley, then evacuated again to a hotel. My mother allowed Shirl and I to go to the cinema to see Five Graves to Cairo, a war film that came out in 1943. We didn't sleep for weeks afterwards because it was so frightening. Perhaps my mother just wanted an afternoon off as being in a hotel with three children must have been quite wearing. Especially since at some point I developed German Measles. The manager said we could stay but only if I was confined to my room. I remember the sounds of the army vehicles rumbling past the hotel.

We went then to live with Auntie Kath, who had been evacuated with her children, Pam and James. This was in the village of Farnham, Dorset at a farm they'd rented. Shirl had long hair, which she wore in plaits and at the boarding school, it was my job to brush and plait it every day. I didn't have time to do it properly as we had to get up and ready at quite a pace. By the time we escaped to Aunt Kath's, it took a day to untangle it.

Mum just wasn't around. She wasn't around for big parts of my life really. I missed her but it was just what happened, and I accepted it at the time. Reflecting on it now, I feel sad. And angry. But that's how it was for me, and a whole generation.

Shirl then went to live with our mother, and I went back to the boarding school. I was relived not to be responsible for Shirl and to be away from the craziness – even though I didn't know what was crazy. If anyone had asked me what was crazy about my family, I wouldn't have known what to say. But I had a sense, that I was an outsider and not part of things. I still feel that to an extent. Maybe it's because I didn't have a secure attachment with my mother.

After this I think we went to stay at Senior's Farm in Semley, Dorset, owned by a Dr Hankey. He was letting it out as he had gone to war. There was fun to be had on the farm for children. So much was new to us, such as hearing someone shout, "Keep the children away!" That was on the days when the bull was brought in to service the cows. Or if a lady called Queenie was there to kill the chickens by wringing their necks. My father occasionally came to visit. He tried to wring a chicken's neck – very easy he thought – until one of the birds just ran away from him, unwinding its neck.

My sister and I had riding lessons from a lady who lived in Semley village. Her cottage had the largest cobwebs I had ever seen. I must have expressed my horror because she told me they kept the flies away! The horse-riding lessons were very relaxed, we learned how to sit the wrong way round, how to fall off properly. Shirl enjoyed it much more than I did.

Aunt Kath came to the farm with my cousin, Pam, a baby at the time. Kate has since told me that when she was feeding Pam in bed at night, there were mice running along the back of her bed. Lots of mice and no central heating seems to be the family's main memory of that time period.

Both sets of grandparents came to stay at the farm with us. We had obviously taken some furniture with us, including my mother's bed and she was furious that my father's father, Grandpa Marriott, drilled a hole in the headboard, so that he could attach a light for bedtime reading. Rationing of food was in full force and my mother gave the food out each week. Her father-in-law would then accuse her of giving more to her own father. I never heard her complain.

The weekly rations, per person, were:
2oz butter
4oz bacon
4oz margarine
8oz sugar
3 pints milk
2oz cheese
1 egg
2oz tea
1lb jam every two months

Bertha, our maid, came with us to assist with running the house. And my mother – bless her heart, she tried so hard – home-schooled us. She took it all very seriously, even taking a register and asking, "Is Jean here? Is Shirley here?" I laugh when I think about it now. There was a strict timetable that included playtime and lunchtime but the whole pantomime never lasted long!

You could wander very safely in those days, so when we weren't otherwise occupied, that's what Shirley and I did. My mother was quite worried about the Italian prisoner of war camp nearby and told us, "I want you girls to remember that if anybody ever comes up to you and says that they've got a message from me, don't take any notice unless at the end of the sentence I name which month it is." It was a great idea, to have a code word like that. And one day when Shirl and I were out roaming, the station master approached Shirl and I and said, "Your mother says you've got to go home." We both looked at him and waited and waited but there was no mention of the month, so we didn't go home. It was the only time that we were ever put to the test and our mother forgot to use the code word. I can't remember why she needed us, probably just because tea was ready, but that sums her up. That absolutely sums her up.

Many strange and some awful things happened during this time and often, the war was given as an excuse. It's interesting to contemplate that my mother was worried about someone outside of the home hurting us. Research shows that it's often the people in our homes and families who, while hiding in plain sight, can be the real danger. And it's not just children who suffer.

Adults were preoccupied, dealing with the worry of the war and family members fighting around the world. My father's younger brother Bill was a captain in the Army, serving mostly in the Middle East. His stepbrother Doug was also an Army captain, serving in Germany and Belgium where he was awarded the MC (Military Cross), although he did come to stay with us when he was on leave. His other stepbrother Malcolm was in the RAF, posted mainly to Texas. Maida was a VAD nurse, a Voluntary Aid

Detachment nurse, trained by the British Red Cross and served on troop ships.

I wasn't frightened of the war, but I must have sensed the uncertainty in the air and perhaps heard hushed adult conversations. What certainly would have been confusing was the fact that I was constantly moving about and separated a great deal from both my parents. I was responsible for Shirl for a great deal of the time we were away from home. It was a lot to ask of a child, but I accepted what had to be done. I didn't have a voice, and, in any case, there was a war on, and everybody had to do what was required.

CHAPTER FOUR

My father and I, stood on the landing of our home in Bromley, watched as a machine we'd never seen before flew over our house making a strange and very loud buzzing sound. There was silence, it fell to earth and then there was a deafening explosion. It was, of course the V1, known as the Doodlebug, a jet-propelled flying bomb, thousands of which were sent into London by the Germans from June 1944. It was like a small airplane, with wings but no pilot. They flew at up to 400kph until they ran out of fuel then they landed and exploded.

We had stayed on the farm for a while and then, before the war was over, we moved back to the house we had moved to in Park Avenue, Bromley. It wasn't totally safe, but my mother was fed up with being away from my father and, like everyone else, wanted some normality.

To protect us from bombs, we had a large

Morrison shelter – essentially an indoor cage – installed in the cellar. When we went to sleep, we had to fold our clothes and place them on the end of our beds, so if the air raid siren sounded, we could get up, grab our clothes and gas masks, and run down to the cellar. My sister always took her favourite dress with her. It was pale turquoise with purple ribbon smocking on the front. Bertha lived in, so she would be in the shelter too. She and my mother cooked there on a small gas cooker.

It was quite fun and actually most of it was quite jolly from my point of view, except when the house of my friend who lived next door was hit by an incendiary bomb and all her Arthur Ransome books were destroyed. This to me was terrible. Fortunately, I don't remember anybody getting really hurt. I recall being told about the butterfly bombs that were in the hedges. We weren't to touch them. And having to carry our gas masks to school. It's amazing what children just accept. This is why they are vulnerable, of course.

Despite my memories of Doodlebugs, Morrison shelters and butterfly bombs, the bombing of London had eased a lot which meant that Shirl, Bill and I could go to school. Shirl and I went to private school, Kinnaird Park, although they very nearly didn't accept us because my father wasn't a professional person. We left after a while as my parents found the fees too much. We were sent to a convent but when we learned nothing there, we returned to Kinnaird Park. Quite honestly, educating Shirl and I was a lost cause. We'd been to so many schools that we didn't really stand a chance of learning anything at all. Countless children in my generation experienced the same. It should also be mentioned that we were taught by older, retired teachers as the younger ones were fighting in the war, so that affected us. Perhaps some of the teachers who had come out of retirement were not up to date and might have been less than pleased to find themselves back in the classroom. Maybe they had sons serving in the war and were distracted. There was Miss Fairbairn who taught English, Miss Moles who taught maths and Miss Forth who was our headmistress. They seemed ancient to us.

I was good at sport but very little else and was finally diagnosed with dyslexia in my 70s after some of my daughters and granddaughters were diagnosed and it dawned on me that I might be in the same boat. It runs in families, and I recall my Aunt Kath who was a bright, intelligent lady always having a dictionary nearby because she said she couldn't spell. Others in the family struggled with spelling too.

My school reports were full of comments about how I didn't concentrate – a sign of dyslexia. I know that if someone tells me how to do something, I just don't retain it – I have to write it down. It's not always a reading issue as was once thought, but a comprehension one. It's a learning difficulty as opposed to a learning disability. I was once in a shop with one of my daughters and she said to the assistant, "I'm sorry but I'm dyslexic and you're going to have to write that down for me." I thought that was an excellent idea and I've done it many times since. Many people say, "Oh, so am I!" When I did my diploma in psychotherapy, I had to get someone else to help me put sentences together. Dyslexia and a wartime education for you!

Schools pick these things up so fast now, and they offer such support. At school, I did what people with any kind of learning difficulty do and I became not exactly the class clown but a bit noisy and extrovert – which was also what you had to be to fit in with my wider family. I think that upset me more than anything when I was diagnosed, that realization that I had possibly adapted my personality to deal with something that I wasn't aware of. Of course, you do it subconsciously, but I can't help wondering what would have been different if either I hadn't been dyslexic, or if I'd been born at a different time and having the help that my grandchildren are getting now. But I just think whatever was meant to be at that time, was meant to be. I'm very philosophical about that. Over the years, my dyslexia has made me a little bit uncomfortable about joining things. I have sense that I'll not be able to do some things.

Outside of school there was much to enjoy. We

had dogs, cats and chickens. My father bought a gun to shoot a rat that was killing the chickens. He never got it of course. We played cards, we played games, and the piano – such a different time when you look at how families spend their leisure time today.

I caught measles and had to stay in my bedroom at one point. All the bedrooms had little fires, so it was nice and cosy. Grandma Johnson came round to sit in my bedroom and knit. It was lovely to doze off and wake up to find her there knitting. I can't remember my mother being there, she would be far too busy sorting the world out somewhere else. I have other lovely memories connected with Grandma Johnson, such as doing embroidery with her; a hobby which became a sanctuary for me for decades. She also took me to Christ Church, on Highlands Road in Bromley. I never understood what the sermon was all about, but Grandma would pass me little iron geloid tablets to help my boredom.

I don't have any memories of the end of the war except a lot of cheering and flags being displayed in the front garden. My paternal grandparents did throw a Christmas party to celebrate all their children – Bill, Doug, Maida and Malcolm – coming home safely. My mother made me a long dress. I was 16 and not impressed with her choice, which I thought was dreadful.

At 11.45pm, Shirl was put in a large, cardboard box which was somehow wheeled into the bathroom at 11.55. And at midnight, she was told to burst out of the top. Happy New Year!

* * *

In the Park Avenue house, Shirl and I started to notice there was a lot of drinking and partying going on – mainly family and some hangers one. My mother would play the piano with my father singing along beside her. It looked as if everyone was having a great time and Shirl and I became convinced that this was the case.

A lot of the partying was due to the war, I'm sure. People needed to let their hair down. It's just that my family always seemed to go a bit over the top. After the war, one Christmas, the whole family went to a hotel. There was a lot of out-of-control fun, for example changing around all the shoes left outside bedrooms for cleaning. The family had to be asked to leave the dance floor at the end of the evening but some of them continued to play some instruments. One relation was very good at playing the drums and had to be told, very sternly, to stop.

There were no boundaries, ever. I was to see over time that if the people closest to me felt anything uncomfortable at all, they would take a pill, have a drink, have an affair or have a party. That's how everything was dealt with. When Bill was in bed asleep, Shirl and I would sit on the stairs and watch and listen.

CHAPTER FIVE

Christmas 1948

Christmas is in full swing. Twenty-two people expected. Extra tables have been added to both ends of dining room table, chairs have been collected from around the house, a plaid blanket has been placed on a wooden plank of wood which had been placed between two chairs for the children.

Family presents had been exchanged earlier but guests were invited at 11.30 to exchange presents and to share in the midday toast to absent friends – a ritual started during the war. Gin and Tonic, Sherry or soft drinks had been offered.

Christmas decorations, many handmade, long paper chains, holly and mistletoe decorated the wooden panelled dining room, and of course the obligatory and beautifully decorated Christmas tree stood in pride of place in the sitting room.

At 1pm sharp, all were called for lunch. Crackers were pulled whilst waiting for the food to arrive, causing much laughter at the small gifts and funny cracker jokes.

What lives at the bottom of the sea and shivers?

A nervous wreck!

What is black and white and noisy?

A Zebra with a drum!

Jokes in Christmas crackers are not really meant to be funny, but groan producing. The bigger the groan the better the joke.

A cosy aroma of Brussel sprouts, stuffing and roasted parsnips drifted in from the kitchen. Most vegetables like potatoes, carrots, parsnips and sprouts were home-grown and eggs were collected daily from the chicken hutches, and there was a shortage of cheese for quite some time.

There was much fun and laughter, as with due pomp and ceremony the succulent looking turkey was carried to the table. Red and white wine was offed at the table while the children had lemonade. Grandfather Johnson, it was noticed, had already indulged in one-too-many gins, but readily accepted red wine when offered.

After the main course was cleared away, in came the flaming Christmas pudding containing surprise sixpence pieces. A tipsy trifle and mince pies were also offered. Grandfather poured an excessive amount of cream over his pudding and was heard to say, "Oh sorry, someone brushed my arm." Everyone laughed as this little performance occurred every year.

After months of planning food, saving up food coupons (as many products were still being rationed) new clothes were being homemade as a new dress simply had to be worn on Christmas day. Best china was washed and dried for the big day. The children had been learning new poems and practising the piano for the afternoon entertainment.

A delicious lunch had been enjoyed by all.

"More gravy please."

"No more sprouts, thank you."

"Sorry I spilt the drink!" were all part of the day. Mother's voice could be heard occasionally saying, "Hold your knife properly, and don't turn your fork over to eat your peas." Then Grandma was heard to say, "Oh, leave them alone on Christmas Day," whereupon a grateful smile passed between her and the children.

Christmas lunch now over, and the adults retired to the lounge for coffee, a liqueur and cigarettes, while the children entertained themselves for a short while. The unfortunate few were cleaning up in the kitchen and at the same time laying the trolley for tea. This was done with much merriment and laughter. All had to be tidied and prepared in time for the King's Speech at 3pm.

Everyone gathered in the lounge, most still

wearing his or her coloured paper hats and sat on anything that was available, most children on the floor, ready to listen. Grandfather always stood whilst the National Anthem was played and frowned at anyone who giggled, as most of the children did.

The grandparents retired for a rest at this time, and others walked the dogs, while others just relaxed chatting. Tea with Christmas fruitcake is served around 4.30pm accompanied by the prepared and much rehearsed entertainment, usually by the children, of piano recitals, poems, or singing. Occasionally, with Mother at the piano a general sing along is enjoyed. She also accompanied Father singing Bless This House.

I remember a poem I learnt for this Christmas afternoon:

A very small cat with a very big bow
Walked up and down, so stuck up you know,
But one day I tell you, she gave no more airs
She tripped on her bow and fell down the stairs.
Her mother was sorry, but what could she do?
Pride must have a fall; we all know that's true.

After tea, which again the unfortunate few had to clear up, sandwiches were made ready to be eaten later if required. There was usually a short pause in activities at this time, but about 6.30 pm alcoholic drinks were offered, then the evening activities began – games like charades, some played bridge, canaster, while the children played hide and seek or played cards, or with their new toys.

Grandparents usually went home or if staying the night, retired at 10pm. Other sundry relatives and cousins gradually departed. At last my parents sat quietly alone in front of the fire, with just the Christmas Tree lights on and had, "One for the road," although their road was only up the wooden hill.

Another fun, delicious, enjoyable, family Christmas day was coming slowly to an end.

CHAPTER SIX

"How's Bill?"

"He died this morning."

That was how I said it. Just like that.

It was day my darling baby brother had died, and I was on a bus. Why was I on a bus? Was I alone? Why was no one taking care of me? My brother had died. Someone asked me and I answered. Heart breaking.

* * *

Sometime before the war ended, we moved from 39, Park Avenue to number 27 in the same road. This had been my paternal grandparents' home, but they had gone permanently to their home in Worthing. Number 27 was lovely house, and even had a tennis court.

Just before we moved in, my mother had a stroke. I was in the house and Dad came in from the garden to say that she had fallen off a ladder. The doctor came to our house and confirmed that she had had a stroke. She was nursed at home. Shirley and I went to stay with our maternal grandparents for a couple of months. More upheaval.

After the stroke, my mother had a weakness in her left hand and a blind spot in her left eye. She could also no longer dance. Or at least she felt that she couldn't. She didn't walk with a limp although she did have a walking stick. Maybe she felt self-conscious. I'm not sure in which month she had her stroke, but I do remember that the following Christmas she came downstairs for Christmas lunch, but after half an hour said, "I can't do this," and went back upstairs to bed.

Unfortunately, due to the war and us moving about so much, I don't have many memories of my Bill as a little boy. I was seven when he was born and when he was 10 and we were back in London, he went to Ardingley College in Haywards Heath. This was the boarding school that my father attended, and my parents were terribly proud of this. Bill jokingly referred to Shirl and me as his ugly sisters and while he was away, he sent birthday cards and letters addressed to My two darling ugly sisters. He was a lovely young man and very much the apple of my mother's eye.

The loss of Bill was a heart-shattering tragedy from which our family never recovered. He came home from school one holiday and my mother noticed his tummy was quite large. She took him for tests, and he was diagnosed with cirrhosis of the liver. Over several months, he gradually became more unwell. He never complained, Bill, bless him, but he must have been in terrible pain as his condition deteriorated. His stomach would fill with fluid and would have to be tapped off, which meant it was drained with a large needle.

We managed to have some good times. I have some lovely pictures of him playing in the garden, with a hose. He's in a wheelchair, spraying Shirl and me. He had a wonderful sense of humour. But nobody thought to speak to Shirl and I about what was happening. I felt as if I was acting in a play, and I watched as my parents aged 100 years in three months. My mother tried everything to help Bill, even calling in a faith healer at one point. But in June 1960, Bill, aged just 11, died at home. My mother and Grandma Johnson were with him. He was in a small room downstairs that had French windows leading onto the garden. I was in the dining room, sat at the table, with my father who was sitting on the windowsill and my grandmother came in and said, "It is all over."

I'm not sure where Shirl was. Parts of this time are a foggy to me, probably because of the trauma. But other things I remember vividly, such as getting on a bus and seeing someone I knew.

Horrifyingly, on the day of the funeral, my sister and I who were just babies really, aged 15 and 17 were told. "No crying now girls, no crying. Stiff upper lip." Barbaric when you think about it. I didn't even cry in private; I don't think. That was the level I was operating on then. I was hardly existing. That's how we lived. Life felt fast, as if there was no time to absorb the feelings of it all.

I'm amazed that Shirl and I didn't react more dramatically to Bill's death than we did. I think we were both just hanging on in there. Many years later she told me that she used to go down to the cemetery to Bill's grave and talk to him about the animals we had at home.

One abiding memory of Bill's death is of a huge number of flowers in our house. Maybe they were condolence flowers, because otherwise they would have been sent to the funeral parlour. But the house was absolutely full, and the perfume lingered for months. Or at least, I could smell it for months. After Bill died, my mother, my sister and I went to northern France for a week's holiday. As we walked along the front, the same scent overwhelmed me. "Can you smell something?" I asked Mum and Shirl, but they couldn't. You hear about that happening, don't you? Because the memory is very connected to the sense of smell.

* * *

After the loss of their son, my parents didn't know how to help each other one bit. Mum wanted to talk about Bill all the time, but Dad didn't. So, if Mum spoke about Bill he walked out of the room. They dealt with it in completely different ways.

His death was devastating on many levels but not least because my parents wanted a boy to carry on the firm. When both my sister Shirley and I were born there was disappointment, but when Bill was born, the flags went out and there were parties.

A year after Bill's death, Shirl developed epilepsy, which I feel was repressed grief. I remember vividly how she collapsed at the breakfast table, and I rang to telephone the doctor and told him, "I think Shirl has died."

The family parties paused for a while after Bill's death. My father was a mason and there were parties that took place as part of that. I enjoyed the ladies' nights at Grosvenor House but one time, not long after Bill's death, I was too frightened to go in. "Don't worry, darling, I'll take you home," my father said. But I insisted that I should be brave.

Even as the decades went on, no one realized that Shirl and I had also been heartbroken by the loss of our darling little brother. Many years later, not long before Aunt Kath died, she said of that time, "Oh, it was a terrible time for Don and Con," referring to my parents.

"It wasn't much fun for Shirley and me, you know," I told her.

"No, no, no but for Don and Con..." she continued. It was as though children don't grieve. "Children should be seen and not heard." This 15th century proverb, as said by a clergyman referring mainly to girls, was still dominating society and child rearing. I felt more invisible than ever.

It wasn't long after Bill died that my father said something to me that changed how I saw myself. "You're my rock of Gibraltar," he said. It would be years before I realised that I didn't want to be my father's rock of Gibraltar. I wanted him to be my rock of Gibraltar. I needed him to be that for me. But at the time, I finally felt seen. When a parent says that to you, you fluff your feathers and feel good. It was meant as a compliment. But I did realise, decades later, that was too much for a child. I feel deeply emotional this, the realization that I had no sense of self at all, that I felt existed to prop up other people.

CHAPTER SEVEN

I stared at my parents. "I heard you say you're going to leave each other," I told them. They had started arguing. Something they never did before Bill died.

"We're not going to do that, are we Connie?" My father kissed my mother. I knew it was for my benefit.

After Bill's death, my parents started taking Valium and a sleeping tablet called Mogadon. My father also started to have affairs with our adult maids. Bertha was no longer with us so other women came to work for us. Sometimes my mother employed teenage girls from broken homes – those who needed to be looked after – my Mum's calling. One I remember was June, an absolute darling and a real cockney. Her parents had split up and she and her older sister and brother had all been put into care. June came to us and stayed for a long time. Another girl, Ena, was pregnant with twins. She was the daughter of a vicar from north of England who had sent her away in disgrace to have the babies and have them adopted.

It was typical of my mother, always finding lost causes, a project. If there wasn't a drama, she'd create one so that she had something to sort out. That was absolutely how she was. Her whole sense of self was tied up with that. That was where she felt useful. My grandmother told me that before she was married, my mother would go down the road and help a family who had lots of children. My grandmother said, "I'd wish Con would help at home like she does down there." Around this time, my uncle Doug was having marital problems with his first wife Peggy. They had two boys, my cousins, and they came to live with us for a while. That was after Bill died, so maybe that helped my mother, to have her nephews come and stay.

The stroke didn't change my mother's personality, but the death of Bill did. It changed her and her marriage. I can't remember if my mother told me about my father's affairs. I never confronted him, but I do remember a party he and I went to. My mother didn't want to go. Before we got there, he said, "I won't tell on you, and you don't tell on me." I took it as a compliment, him taking me into his confidence. I didn't do anything that he could have divulged to my mother anyway – a minor flirtation.

At least my father, I would think later, wasn't going

around the family like the others were. He was grieving. But I wonder why my mother didn't leave, although I know at that time that this was uncommon. And she was fragile in many ways. Apparently, she said to my Grandpa Marriott one day, "You've just got to speak to Don, I can't go on like this." His reply was, "It's your marriage, you sort it out." But she had no idea how.

It was around the time that an uncle began to say things to me such as, "I wish you weren't my niece." Everyone thought he and his younger brother were most amusing. Opposite us, lived a woman with three daughters, the eldest called Eileen. One of them fancied her. He had binoculars in his bedroom and would watch Eileen getting undressed. Everyone laughed about it, so even though I felt uncomfortable, I thought it was normal. All apart from the tiniest part of me. Insidious. I began to wish that I knew someone, a relative, who lived far away. I would say to myself, if only I knew someone living a long way away and I could go and live with them. My family made me feel hemmed in. Everyone seemed to know everything. If I even sneezed, it felt as if the whole family were talking about me having a cold. I think too, that I wanted to put psychological boundaries in place between the inappropriate actions of certain members of the family. And of course, the emotional wound that was the loss of Bill.

In my late teens, I was lonely, and I would go for

long walks, which I understand now can be a response to trauma. I became friendly with the porter at Shortlands Station, and he was the first person who kissed me. He was nice looking and enjoyed chatting together. It was quite exciting, and safe, and innocent. Was it a nice first kiss? Maybe. But also, I see again how I was drifting and had no sense of self. I had no friends of about my age and feel it's so sad that I ended up kissing this stranger while out on my solitary walks.

CHAPTER EIGHT

I achieved nothing at school, and I didn't know what I wanted to do with my life. My mother tried to help me, and I ended up going to a hairdressing college in London where I trained as a hairdresser and manicurist. By 1951, I was working at the Savoy hotel and Claridge's as a manicurist. One evening, I was asked to go in specially to give a manicure to the film producer Sir Alexander Korda, the first filmmaker to receive a knighthood in 1942. My father insisted on taking me and waiting for me to take my home. The tip Sir Alexander gave me was four times the cost of the manicure! But my heart wasn't in it, so my mother suggested nursing – an absolute blessing. I couldn't train at a London hospital because I didn't have enough exam results, but Bromley Cottage hospital took me on, and I trained there from 1951 to 1955.

Bromley Cottage was a small hospital with four

wards, plus a casualty department and outpatients. It was like a village – the surgeons would come onto the ward on Christmas Day to carve the turkey! It was fun and I learned a lot about life. I loved the camaraderie and felt truly safe for the first time. There was discipline and we had boundaries – so different from my home life. I felt relaxed, knowing exactly what was expected of me. Not all of it came naturally. We were due to learn how to give injections by practicing on an orange. I was dreading it so much that I hid in a cupboard, and I could hear the sister saying, "Where's Nurse Marriott? Where is she?" I came out in the end, and it all went fine.

We moved from ward to ward to learn as much as we could. And we would always be moved if relatives came into the hospital. We were not allowed to treat relatives. However, something must have gone wrong with that system because I nursed Shirl after she had her appendix out. I was so nervous. I had to give her an injection and it was the worst one I ever did.

It was between December 5 and 9, 1952, that The Great London Smog descended – smog being a mixture of the words smoke and fog. It had been exceptionally cold for weeks, meaning more coal was being burned to warm homes. Then an area of high pressure came in over southern England, which trapped the cold air below. Every day, thousands of tons of soot were pumped into the air from factories, coal fires in homes and from vehicles. With no wind and no escape upwards, the soot-laden smog became a 30-mile-wide poisonous stew. You couldn't see your hand in front of your face. London ground to a halt with trains, buses and cars were unable to move. When I needed to get to the nurses' home, my father walked me there. I held his arm and remembered how very silent and eerie it all felt. It has only just occurred to me that he would have had to walk back again! It wasn't until undertakers began to run out of coffins and florists out of flowers that the impact of the smog was realised. It's now believed that 12,000 people died.

I was training to become a state registered nurse, but I failed my exam, which was devastating. I thought that my colleagues weren't studying and that I didn't need to either. Some of the other girls who failed didn't consider retaking their exam and just left. I couldn't believe how anybody could leave after all the terrible jobs we'd done with nothing to show for it! I was determined to do another six months and re-take my exam.

The day I got my original results, I went into an outpatient ENT clinic and there was a Mr Broad, consultant, and he said, "You look a bit miserable this morning, Nurse z."

"I've just failed my finals."

"Never mind, all the best nurses fail once," he told me.

It was a lovely thing to say, and I could have kissed him. Then I passed. It was the first thing I'd really achieved. My mother sent me a telegram of congratulations, which was lovely.

One unexpected and super result of my nursing training was that my stutter disappeared, probably because I was busy and distracted. I made some wonderful friendships at the hospital, much healthier than the friendships I had at school where I felt everyone was much cleverer than me, something of a barrier.

My mother was really struggling at that time. She was on uppers, downers and drinking too much. I lived in at the hospital which was lovely but invariably my father would say, "Can you just come home for a week?" So, I'd go home about every six weeks. My mother would calm down when I was there. I'd talk to her and get into bed and just hold her until I felt her relax.

My sister's epilepsy was bad at that time, and she was very ill while the medics worked to get her medication right. Having lost one child, my mother was obsessed with looking after Shirl. This was completely understandable, but the house became divided. It was my mother and Shirl and then my father and me. There I was, my father's rock and comforting my mother. I think my mother felt safe with me because I appeared independent and was doing well out in the world.

My parents still had their parties. At times my mother seemed normal, and at other times, she wasn't. But she continued to arrange parties, which she loved doing and was very good at. They always got out of hand, which everyone considered great fun. Doug and Malcolm were going skiing one year and since everyone was completely drunk, they tied brooms to their feet as skis and guests began shaking soap suds over them to replicate snow and get them in the mood. There were three chairs broken. Anything went.

Two of my friends came to one of our parties and afterwards, the friendship cooled off. I wonder now if this was because something happened with the uncles. It seems likely.

* * *

I had a nice social life outside of nursing. There was a gang of us, girls and boys, all of us a similar age and similar background. I'm not sure how we all met, maybe through hockey team that Shirl played in. The gang played hockey and tennis and the boys of the group had their own skiffle band. We met in the music department of the Medhurst department store in Bromley on a Saturday morning where we played the latest records. We'd go to the pub opposite to arrange where we were going to meet that night.

It was fun, but I felt as if I was tagging on. I never

felt carefree or part of the gang. My sister did. She worked as a receptionist at my father's firm. My mother didn't want her to go too far away in case she blacked out. My mother over-managed Shirl, you could say. She rang up to check on her wherever she went. But despite this, Shirl had very free spirit and could be the centre of attention on half an orange juice. I was jealous and wondered how she did it. She got us into the competitor's enclosure at Wimbledon once. She told me, "Just keep walking and look confident!" And it worked! Shirl was an amazing woman actually, very courageous. I wish I'd known her better.

After I qualified, I worked nights at the hospital for a year. By then I'd met my husband, Rick Swales, who was training to be an accountant. He was living at home with his parents who had just returned to England following Rick's father's work in India. I invited him home to play tennis, just as friends, and he and my mother got on famously and organized a tournament at our house. Around this time, a friend of Rick's invited me to a party. He was a doctor and I told him, "John, you can take me, but I don't guarantee you can bring me home!" I remember being so forward at the time, but I knew Rick would be there, so I wanted to leave my options open.

There was a quietness about Rick and having come from a family where nobody knew what quietness was, I felt safe with him. He brought me home from the party and we began dating. We went out as a crowd mainly, or to the cinema – we mainly saw musicals, and sometimes we went for a drive in the country to a pub. My parents had moved to Keston in Kent by then and there were lots of lovely pubs in the Kent countryside.

Since Rick was in training and we didn't have much money, I began working as a nurse in private houses as the pay was better. I cared for people who could afford private nurses, the elderly who needed general nursing care, or were convalescing. It could be a long day if there wasn't much to do. Some days I was being paid to arrange flowers.

Rick and I got engaged, which lasted for about three years and then we married. I sometimes say it was for the wrong reasons, which sounds harsh but what I mean is that people kept saying to us, "When are you two going to get engaged?" and, "You'll be next!" I think he felt pressurized. I think it's also possible that he noticed that I was taking care of my mother and father emotionally and he wanted to take care of me.

I have written about this situation though, of looking back and wondering if that was right for Rick and me. The culture and social atmosphere of the time very much promoted this as the thing to do. I've spoken to other people of my age, and they said we all got married for the wrong reasons. Bless Rick's heart, I adored him, but maybe he shouldn't have married anybody. He was a Virgo and I'm not saying that unpleasantly, but he was a loner. He didn't need lots of people. He was self-contained, not too loud, a quiet soul. He was brought up an only child in India and loved my crazy family.

The wedding planning was all very unromantic in those days and, as was the pattern of my life, I had no voice. When I see Say Yes To The Dress on television now, I cry with happiness for those brides. It really hits home how much I would loved to have such a say in things, and a mother by my side making it all happen as I desired, rather than as tradition dictated. Maybe they don't last, these weddings, but it seems so romantic and thoughtful, planning it all and friends and loved ones choosing the dress. My mother arranged for a dressmaker to make my dress and I was able to have some say. I was able to choose my headdress, which I loved.

But all credit to my mother since, sadly by this time, my father was very unwell with terminal lung cancer. I don't know how she managed to arrange a wedding in the midst of that, but she did it all. I got ready at my parents' house and have some lovely photographs. Shirl and my cousin Pam were my grown-up bridesmaids and I had three little ones.

Rick and I married on February 8, 1958 at St Mary's Church in Bromley. It was where all the family occasions had taken place – including Bill's funeral – with the same vicar. It was snowing so the

Marriott men arranged for an awning to be erected from the church gate to the entrance.

I've given my wedding day a lot of thought recently. I most certainly did want to marry Rick and I was pleased to be leaving the area where all the family lived. Rick had secured a job at an Esso refinery at Fawley, in the New Forest, in Southampton, so we were moving quite a distance. Our wedding wasn't the best. I took some purple hearts that I'd found at home. What can I say? It wasn't the first time I'd done it. They just made me feel better, more alive. I wasn't nervous. I found them and I took them.

The reception was at Bromley Court Hotel. My mother had arranged the food and the cake. Rick and I had our first row while cutting it. He said we should cut the top tier and I said we should cut the bottom so that the cake didn't collapse. There's a photograph of that moment and you can see we're rowing. Rick wouldn't do a first dance with me. I didn't react to that at all. I was used to having no say, of being of very little importance. Many years later he said this was because my mother had told him to, and he said he wasn't going to start married life by being told what to do by his mother-in-law.

But of course, a terribly sad part was my father being so ill. He'd had to have a shot of morphine to be able to walk me down the aisle and he couldn't stay for the whole day, which he regretted because he wasn't able to make a speech. We were driven to the church together, but he was so poorly, going through the motions really. Not that you'd know that from the photographs.

Rick and I drove away from the reception with the traditional tins tied to the back of the car – every wedding was the same in those days. Our honeymoon was two days in London because both our fathers were in hospital – different hospitals – so that was that. We stayed at the Cumberland Hotel and walked around. It was February, so too cold to do much.

But despite a slightly bumpy start, somehow, Rick and I made it work despite all our differences. There were lots of ups and downs. He broke off our engagement at some point, then asked me again to marry him which I did, probably because my father was dying, which was also more than likely why he proposed.

I find lovely cards around. I found some the other day in which he'd written that I was the best thing that had ever happened to him and how we had three beautiful daughters, and that he'd had a lovely life.

47 years, we were together.

CHAPTER NINE

Our house in the New Forest was tiny, but I thought it was the most amazingly wonderful house that I'd ever seen in my life. I just adored it. I was thrilled to have finally got away from the toxicity of my family. I knew in my heart and soul that there was something not right. I couldn't put my finger on it. But my soul knew and was scared.

But despite the relief of being so far away from it all, once I settled in the New Forest, I became very bored. Rick was working, our tiny house took barely any time to clean, and the nearest village was quite far away. I hadn't passed my driving test, but I would go to the garage, take the car out and then put it back, and then take it out and go a bit further, and then put it back. The garages where the local residents kept their cars were at the top of the road. Rick used a carpool to go to work. I didn't go further than the village, but I remember I was at a party once and somebody said, "Jean, when are you going to pass your test?" To think people were talking about it! I thought, I jolly well need to do something about this. So, I took the test, failing it the first time. The examiner had a broken leg and I wanted to break the other one, I was that cross. I expect I was overconfident because I'd been driving for so long.

But I passed and filled my days driving about and sorting the garden. We were the first people there as the house was newly built, and the garden was like a builders' site. I don't remember what I did to make it better, but I do recall the first roast dinner I cooked. I wrote to my father to tell him. "Isn't married life so exciting!" I was genuine. Rick and I had very little money and a treat was to share a bottle of cider while playing cards with the neighbours. I stopped taking purple hearts. There were none around, so it didn't cross my mind.

I did go and see my father as much as I could and sometimes Rick came too. In the end my father became suspicious as to the regularity of my visits because I don't think he actually knew he was dying. As was typical for my family, we hadn't spoken about it. He died in June 1958, four months after my wedding. I was at my parents' home when my father passed but sadly, when the moment came, Shirl and I had popped to the chemist's.

His funeral took place at the church where my marriage had taken place just a few months beforehand. In those days the men of the family went to the burial in the cemetery, and the women went home to prepare the wake, so that's what we did. Rick and I stayed with my mother for about a few days, then we went home.

I was numb about my father's death. I adored him and I was sad that he wasn't there anymore, but I found it difficult to feel anything. He did his absolute best, but he wasn't the best father. We weren't emotionally close. He depended on me. My mother used to say when we were little, "Don't worry if your father doesn't seem that interested, he will be when you're older." But he never was. He didn't take much notice, not of our interests or our schooling. I suppose our times apart during the war didn't help, then the illness and death of Bill.

Materially, he would give me anything I needed. I would find cheques under my pillow in my teenage years. It might have been if I'd mentioned a pretty dress I'd seen, or something like that. I learned later, during my therapy training, many men who can't give of themselves emotionally, might be more comfortable to give you things materially.

* * *

I think Rick might have wanted me to himself for a while longer, but Jules was on her way. My pregnancy was perfectly normal. I was hooked on chewing coal.

57

Luckily, we had a coal fire, so I had a steady supply. I only had one maternity dress so I washed it overnight so I could wear it daily. You might not believe that, but it's the truth – I can picture it now. It was a very hot summer, so coal washed down with ice was my diet.

Jules was born on July 10, 1959. Now that I had passed my test, I would drive up to see Mum. But our little sports car would have been incredibly impractical with a baby, so Mum bought us a Morris Minor when I was eight months pregnant. We weren't best pleased, but it would have been ridiculous to say we wouldn't have it and it turned out to be an amazing little car. I didn't see my mother a great deal once I moved to Southampton, but I did pop up to Kent with the children in the car, on my own, quite happily to visit. That was always an extraordinary experience because she was always so disorganised. She had a cleaner who came in occasionally but that was all. I noticed at this stage that she was drinking more than she had been.

Jules had colic as a baby and was very unsettled, which might have been more to do with me than her. I see these baby slings mothers have these days and think that I would have loved to have one of those. I followed a baby book by a man called Dr Benjamin Spock who was very hot on routines. It was all the rage at the time. But once Jules grew out of the colic, she was the darlingest baby.

Catherine, known as Kate, came next, two and a half years later, born on February 20, 1962. I think Jules felt a bit pushed out and that I didn't make a fuss of her when she came to the hospital to meet her baby sister. I think that's quite a common feeling for second children – or at least it was then. I think these days that parents are much more aware of the needs of siblings when a new baby arrives.

After Kate was born, my mother insisted on coming to stay in our tiny home and wanted to bring her housekeeper. It was absurd. They had a room each and Rick and I were in our bedroom with Jules on a camp-bed and Kate in a cot. We nearly went mad and were pleased when she got a cold and decided to go home so that she didn't give us all her germs. With a house that tiny, one didn't need a mother and a housekeeper – typical of her really.

Kate wasn't very impressed with her third birthday present, the arrival of Sarah on exactly the same day three years later in 1965! When I was pregnant with Sarah, my mother came down to help me with the children because Rick had moved to the Midlands. He had started a new job and was looking for a house for us. But my mother was impossible because she was so worried about Shirl who was pregnant with Simon at the same time. One day I said to her, "Just go and stay with Shirl."

"Are you sure?" she asked me, but she was virtually packing as she spoke. It was actually quite a relief when she went.

In 2019, Sarah, Jules and I visited the area where the cottage was. I wanted to go inside but they didn't. We took photographs of the hospital where they were born. Honestly, it was like looking back on another life. I loved motherhood, absolutely loved it. But I am able to be honest and say that when the girls were young, I didn't feel as connected to them as I do now. I think that's possibly because my mother and I weren't securely attached, so I didn't know how to create that attachment between the girls and myself. I'm so grateful that I've lived long enough to develop my relationship with them.

But that's not to say that we didn't have many happy times. When the girls were small, I loved taking them into the forest. I had a friend who had her own daughter and dog and we had walks and picnics together. It was an idyllic place to have children.

Kate and Julie played nicely together. Julie adored Kate. We played snakes and ladders and those sorts of games. There wasn't much children's television in those days, just Andy Pandy and The Magic Roundabout. They were left to their own devices in a lot. They had friends and went in and out of their houses and played.

I took them to visit my Mum about three times a year. There were parties, of course, and they were introduced to my family from an early age.

CHAPTER TEN

My mother's death in 1968 came completely out of the blue. It's still hard to think about. Doug rang Rick at work, and Rick came home to tell me. For about a month, I believed what I had been told, which was that she died of a heart attack and been found dead in her bed. Then my Aunt Kath realised that I should know what happened and told me the truth. My mother had died from an accidental overdose of barbiturates and alcohol.

Aunt Kath was devastated because there was an inquest, but she wasn't told about it. A relation called into her house and told her the outcome. She said, "Well why didn't you tell me? I would have liked to have come!"

"I didn't think it would be a good idea," he told her. They were like the Mafia, those men. Ironically given the damage they did, they thought they were protecting their women in making that sort of decision.

There was a large article about my mother's death in the local paper and Aunt Kath sent that to me, which was devastating. I wrote to the editor, asking, "For God's sake, haven't you got something more interesting to write about?" Pathetic really because obviously they were going to write about it. Losing her daughter, and the details being in the paper must have been hard for Grandma Johnson. She lived almost next door to my mother. By then she had lost a daughter, a grandson, two sons-in-law, and all of her brothers and sisters.

Rick, the girls and I went up for the funeral of course and stayed with his parents at their flat in Chislehurst. Mum had bought all the girls a teddy bear when they were babies, so I had a big teddy bear made of yellow flowers from the grandchildren. It sat at the back of the coffin, looking out at us as we followed behind. It was just right. It made everyone smile a little bit when they saw that.

My mother was slightly fragile because she'd had a stroke and she drank but I wasn't expecting her to die. It was typical of her that she would take a sleeping tablet, then if it didn't work quickly enough, she would take another one. I do believe it was an accidental death, not that that helps at all really.

I coped, I suppose, as one does. But I was distraught and the following spring, I felt I had to get away and Ricky booked a caravan in north Wales for a week with friends. It did me the world of good. But I couldn't believe that life could just carry on. I went to the Esso New Year's Eve dance, but I didn't want to enjoy myself and when Auld Lang Syne came on, with those words about forgetting, I had to go outside because I was sobbing. I still find that song hard to listen to. The whole thing was an awful shock. The doctor prescribed me some Valium, which I took for a while.

The children were old enough to realise that their Nana had gone. She was the first important person in their lives to die. One day when we were driving, Sarah said to me, "What's Nana actually wearing now, Mummy?"

"Something long and white," I told her.

* * *

Three years before my mother died, she came up and spent a weekend with us. Afterwards, she told Aunt Kath, "Do you know, I think I've got to know Jean this time for the first time." I wasn't surprised to hear that.

Apparently, Aunt Kath would tell my mum off about the way she treated me. When she told me this in later years, I couldn't think what she was talking about. It hadn't occurred to me that there was anything unusual about the way my mother was towards me. To me it just was the way it was.

I suppose she softened as I got older because on this occasion, her visit had coincided with my birthday and she asked me, "What are you doing for your birthday?"

"I don't know," I said. "Maybe we'll go out for a meal or something,"

"Nonsense!" she said. "Just go off in the car for a couple of hours and when you come back – party!"

Bless her heart, when I came back there was jelly all over the floor in kitchen and she'd spilled everything. But the children were there, and they each had a friend for tea. The dining table was filled with all the typical birthday cake things, and all the children got up and made a speech. It was the sweetest thing really.

* * *

Shirl and Mike married in 1962 and had their children Michael, Simon and Sophie in 1962, 1965 and 1966. They lived in Hampshire in The Wallops – three villages called Over Wallop, Nether Wallop and Middle Wallop. Mike was training to be a pilot at RAF Middle Wallop. It wasn't too far away, but we didn't see much of them at all. We lived such different lives and didn't even meet up socially.

Shirl's epilepsy was mainly controlled by medication, but it came and went, as it depended tremendously how she was; if she was overtired or stressed it got worse. Hers and Mike's marriage wasn't the happiest. It was hard for the children growing up with that. Shirl and I didn't have much in common all our lives, except when we both had three children and I went out to Australia when she was ill. We really talked then. Our lives had been quite separate really, or at least it felt that way.

I'm not too sure which year it was, but Mike became a pilot for Qantas and Shirl and her family moved as well. Mum was upset. She wanted to go and visit but told me she didn't have any money.

"Sell your diamonds!" I said.

"I can't do that!"

"Why? You want to go to Australia? Sell something!" To me they were only diamonds. But she never went.

Shirl came over for my mother's funeral, of course. She and I then had to go through my mother's things. We laughed about the impractical nonsense she planned to take back to Australia. I was shocked at the amount some members of the family took for themselves. There are no pockets in shrouds, as the expression goes. They're all just things, really.

My mother left the girls £200 each. We let Jules spend her money on a horse. You could buy a horse for £200 then. All her friends were going to nightclubs by this time and might have spent the money on clothes and make-up, but the horse was the right decision for Jules. She adored riding. She didn't care how she looked or whether it was raining or anything. She spent all day down at the stables. Kate bought one later, but then she sold it and bought a motorbike. Later she would disappear off on a motorbike to north Wales and I didn't know where she was. Jules also became a biker. Sarah bought a chopper, which was her pride and joy – her freedom.

I inherited one of my mother's diamond watches. It was a beautiful watch but I'm not a diamond watch person, so I sold it and we bought a family caravan. I gave a lot of thought to it. We had great fun in that caravan.

In 1972, for my 40th birthday, Rick and I took the girls to a campsite in south of France – in our caravan. Somehow Rick had taken the girls shopping to buy little pressies and cards, which I still have. I remember four matches being stuck into a very small cake which were lit and blown out, then a wish made, as I cut this very tiny cake.

It was a lovely day and the whole campsite seemed to know it was my birthday which caused much shared laughter.

I remember being fascinated to watch the children from many different countries all playing together. In the midday heat they would gather under our awning to make shell dolls with shells which had been collected from the beach. There were quite a lot of sleepovers going on – children sleeping in friend's caravans. They would go off with pillow under one arm and favourite teddy under the other. Our caravan always seemed to be extra full and one of the mothers said to me, "You know why they all want to come to your van don't you?"

"No," I replied.

"It's because you have chocolate spread!"

It's such a happy memory.

* * *

But before this time, in the 1960s, we had moved to Sutton Coldfield. I hated it. It was so different to the New Forest, very suburban and we were living in quite an affluent area. I'd never been north of Watford. Rick did tell me that quite literally even the grass wasn't the same colour up there and he was right. I didn't find the accent soothing, quite the opposite in fact, and I wasn't pleased when the girls picked it up. Jules had started school, a little country infant school down in Hampshire, and she found the change of school difficult.

But life went on. The girls had dancing classes and went to Brownies and later, Guides. As they progressed through their education, none of the girls enjoyed school. The biggest problem was the huge mix of types of families, and their different upbringings. Some children didn't do their homework. Jules was bullied for doing hers, so she stopped. The girls weren't in top grades, they were in the middle. Rick and I searched high and low for a solution, and I do wonder what might have been different if they'd gone to better schools. I do know that there's no point saying that; they were meant to go where they went. The fact is what they're doing now with their lives is what they are meant to do. So, they all went to university but not until their late twenties, for different reasons.

Rick was away a lot on courses and things but that was no problem to me, really. When he was home, we had a bit more of a social life. We had a little bit more money, we started mixing with people who drank a bit more, and we started to do the same. I inadvertently created the environment that I had so much wanted to escape, lots of people and crazy parties.

When Sarah started school, I went back to nursing. I started doing two nights a week at Good Hope hospital. Rick was furious, or rather he was hurt, because the managers' wives at Esso didn't work and his friends agreed that what I was doing was wrong. They'd ask me, "Jean, why do you want to go to work?"

"Because it's so boring doing housework!" I told them. It was my time off, really, and I just loved it. The first time I returned after a night shift, no-one in the house would talk to me. Rick had brainwashed the girls. It didn't last long. They soon realized that I wasn't giving up. I think it was a good example to set the girls, to show them that mothers are always balancing but that we can make our own decisions and have some independence. I was determined – it was only two nights a week and nobody was inconvenienced, although I did find out later that the girls would sit up worrying about how much their father was drinking. I was aware of Rick drinking heavily, but I didn't realise how much the girls witnessed.

I felt that something had to change so I drove out to the villages and looked around, hoping that we could move out there and find some peace. But Rick wouldn't move. When his mother died, she left us a lot of money and I asked him then if we could move to a village. He said, "No, I'm going to use my mother's money to modernize my house." We got all these gadgets, such as a washing machine and dishwasher, and I had to learn to use them. We had an opening-of-the-new-kitchen party – of course! It was a lovely kitchen in the end and in Rick's defence, our house was just the kind he'd always wanted. He loved it. It was a large, Edwardian property – very much his castle – and he wouldn't leave. But overall, it was all a bit bleak really and it was from there that the girls launched into adulthood, not the healthiest launch pad at all.

CHAPTER ELEVEN

Why not? I thought.

For a long time, Rick had been accusing me of having affairs with anyone and everyone. I don't know why, maybe he had seen an uncle being inappropriate with me and thought that I was the one doing the flirting. I once told him, "I'm not having an affair. But even if I say I'm not, I know you don't believe me."

Peter was someone in our social group and in all honesty, it was just lovely to have him in my life. Of course, I wouldn't have had an affair for no reason. Our marriage was not in a good place. In about 1950, my mother had given me her wedding ring. "You can have that, it never brought me good luck," she told me. About 20 years later, I was driving through Sutton Coldfield on a rainy day, and I thought, I don't want this, so I threw it out of the window. I was going through a patch of unhappiness, and I thought: that bloody ring. So out the window it went.

Rick was obsessed with Esso and his job. One day I managed to get him to agree to take me out for lunch, but he took me for coffee at the pub where he knew his reps would be. Not exactly what I was hoping for. So, I had this affair, on and off from 1974 for four or five years. It was lovely, really. It was so nice to be treated like a woman and to be wanted. It's hard to remember how it all worked. We couldn't text each other to make plans to see each other, so I suppose we phoned on the landline at an appropriate time. I think I just felt safe with Peter; he reminded me of my father. He had his own business. It was just so lovely to have a conversation with somebody who I just felt comfortable with. I never thought we'd leave our spouses. I always referred to his wife as "madam" and he always referred to Rick as "sir".

My only regret is that it caused a lot of pain and upset to the girls. And unfortunately, it was Kate who found the letters that Peter had sent me. I don't remember whether she brought them to me or to Rick. But as it all began to end, I was at a party and Peter's wife said to me, "Do you want my husband?"

And I said, "No. I want my own, but he doesn't want me."

It was all out in the open then. People had known for a while. I suggested to Rick that we went to Relate but we went once and he said, "I'm not going again." We tried some other counselling. I liked it because I enjoyed being in the car with Rick on the journey there and back, just chatting about ourselves. But it didn't really do the trick. And after that Rick and I never talked about it. Can you believe that? We never talked about it. We just carried on.

Sometime later, Aunt Kath – an astute woman – said to me about the letters, "Was it a relief when they were found?"

And I said, "Actually it was."

Peter wanted to go on meeting up even when I moved south, but I knew it wasn't the answer to anything.

* * *

Before we moved away from Sutton Coldfield and when the girls were about eight to 12, Shirl was going through one of her many trial separations from Mike. She came over to England with the children and they went to school with our girls. Whether it was good or not, I don't know. That's how it was. Our home was three storeys, so we were easily able to put them up. They simply took over the top floor of the house. It caused a degree of unrest. My girls said that I spoiled their cousins and maybe I did. But Shirl was so strict. Her children couldn't believe how lenient I was. And it's true, I was. I didn't do boundaries. I let my girls be pretty crazy. After my experience with my mother's over-the-top discipline, I always swore to myself that I would never tie my daughters to my apron strings or be too strict with them. I wanted to be friends with them in a way I never was with my mother. But it all got very confusing for everyone. There were no boundaries, very few rules from me – possibly also to balance the fact that Rick had so many.

When Shirl returned to Australia, she telephoned me a lot. She was distressed and would reverse the charges. The cost, from Australia, was astronomical, and in the end, Rick put a payphone in. I was mortified when friends came over and needed to call their babysitter and had to start rooting about for change! I do understand why he did it and he was right. But in the end, I told him, "Either the payphone goes, or I do."

When Michael was 14, Simon was 12 and Sophie was 10, Shirl became ill with breast cancer. She was divorced from Mike by then, which made everything more difficult. Shirl had needed a mastectomy but had left it too late as Mike was hinting at reconciliation and she thought he wouldn't want her if she'd had a mastectomy. By the time she wanted to go ahead, the cancer had spread.

I went to visit her, believing that I was going to help her get over the mastectomy and move into a new house. We went to the hospital together for what we thought was a routine appointment but instead, the doctor told us that no more could be done. We went outside and sort of collapsed onto the steps and just sat there, utterly stunned. I'd bought us these two mood rings. We put them on, and the colours indicated that we were both calm and tranquil. We cried with laughter because that was the last thing we were.

We really had to work together then, probably for the first time. We didn't really have much in common. We just had to be practical. Shirl was much deeper actually than me, more sensitive. I couldn't leave her out there in Australia. There was no district nurse, nobody to look after her. I made an excuse to go and see her doctor. I told him, "You've got to help me. I've got to make some decisions here. How long do you think my sister has got?"

"Jean you're a nurse, you know," he said.

"That's not helpful, I've got to try and get her back to England if there's nobody out here."

"A year," he said.

I wasn't sure whether to tell Shirl what the doctor had said but then at a later date, as we were driving over the Sydney bridge she said to me, "I wish someone would have the courage to tell me how long I've got."

I took a deep breath, looked out of the window and said, "You've got about six to eight months."

"At last," she said. "At least now I know what to do."

But she didn't. How could she? She went on

pretending until we left Australia. Then we packed up the house, her jewellery, everything. She was beside herself worrying about her children and went round asking all the good people she could think of if they would look after them for her. It was excruciatingly painful. She never asked me though, which was telling. She had seen how Rick and I lived, and it wasn't the environment she wanted for her children. I see that now. She was strict like our mother, the opposite of me. And she didn't like the partying and how often we had people round. Things would often get out of hand.

We arrived back in the UK in May 1976. I had contacted the surgeon who looked after my brother and wrongly assumed that he would be at the airport to collect us. When he wasn't, I didn't know what to do so I called Malcolm and he came for us. He didn't know what to do with us either, so he drove us to Sutton Coldfield to recover from the flight and decide as to what to do next. Shirl began having chemotherapy at the Royal Marsden and would stay with family in London, often Aunt Kath, then come home to our house. I had become so attached to her during our six weeks in Australia that I didn't want anyone else looking after her and I hated letting her go south. Her children came over to see her a few times.

On our flight together to England, Shirl had spoken about going home and what colour she was going to do her bathroom. But by October, it was over. Aunt Kath and I were with Shirl when she died at the Royal Marsden. Doug collected us and then insisted we go for a slap-up lunch at Wheeler's. Extraordinary, and even more extraordinarily, neither Aunt Kath nor I said a word. We just went along with it, the same way I had when he took me to a nightclub after my mother died. Ridiculous. Me, an adult, powerless to say, "No, I don't want to do that." My family thought that if everyone looked as if they were having a good time, then they were.

The funeral was devastating, deeply sad. But I do recall Grandma Johnson sitting next to me and saying in a very loud voice, "Darling, I do like your new shoes!" Everybody who heard it let out a little giggle. It burst the bubble and was just lovely. Afterwards, we went back to Aunt Kath's flat and my girls, especially Jules, were heartbroken to see people treating the occasion as if it was a party. It was so inappropriate so, as soon as we could, we left to drive back to the Midlands. But by then Rick had had too much to drink and it was a terrible journey. The girls were crying, and I was saying, "You've got to stop the car." He didn't.

It was a surreal time. I was operating in a mist of emotion. I think it brought up the loss of Bill, which had been swept under the carpet. I chose the hymn All Things Bright And Beautiful to be played, as it had also been played at Bill's funeral.

When I arranged my sister's burial, I instructed that on the gravestone it should say her name and then say: who has joined her loved ones." Mike was devastated and said, "What are you talking about? We're her loved ones."

I said, "Yes you are." It was an awful mistake that I'd made. But I couldn't change it. I suppose I was thinking of my parents and their three children and what had happened to us all.

Shirl's children weren't brought over from Australia for their mother's funeral, and they never forgave their father for that, particularly Michael, with whom I am very close. They visited us for Christmas after Shirl died. I think they needed to come and see that she really wasn't here. One night I found them laying in bed with the service sheet from her funeral, singing the hymns we had sung – heart-breaking.

Just recently, Michael told me, "Whenever it's a full moon I talk to it and pretend it's Mum." I thought it was so lovely that he can talk to her like that. Simon can't, even mentioning her makes him deeply emotional.

That same year, Malcolm's son Christopher died in a recreational parachuting accident as did Kate's best friend Joanna, who had cancer. A terrible year and inside, I was broken. I had now lost my darling brother, my father, my mother and my sister.

How I carried on, I'll never know.

CHAPTER TWELVE

We could have come back down to London six years before we did. Rick had been offered a job in the capital but refused it without discussing it with me. I discovered this when we were at a work event, and I was dancing with Rick's boss. He knew I wanted to get back to London and asked me how I felt about Rick refusing an offer from the company to do so. I said I knew nothing about it.

"Oh…" he said.

"I was brought up to believe that the happiness of the family was dependent on the happiness of the father and his job," I told him. That was true.

Educationally it would have been much better for the girls to be in London. I worried about Rick's relationship with Jules — that he wasn't always as kind as he could have been. Sarah and Kate say they saw nothing untoward, but I certainly did. We had money worries in a huge house that we couldn't afford, and of course all the drinking and partying took its toll.

It was 1982 when we moved from Sutton Coldfield to Bickley in southeast London. Unfortunately, Kate wouldn't come with us. She didn't want to leave her friends and had started her nursing training at Dudley Road Hospital. She was extremely upset, and I was very worried about her. But there was nothing I could do about it except telephone our family doctor and ask him to keep an eye on her. She suffered deeply as a result. I tried to go up to see her whenever I could, such as when she had exam results due. I was insistent that we had a house with a room for her use only so that it was there for her if she wanted it. Kate would say it couldn't have happened any other way, but I still think about it.

We didn't find a social scene in Bickley. We joined the Roundtable social club, and they were interesting people, but Rick was a shy person. When it came to putting an effort into meeting new folks, he just couldn't be bothered and didn't want to do it. We met a couple of couples who I quite liked but mainly we depended on family. A relative had moved to Wrotham and wanted us to go down there to his parties because, essentially, we were his drinking partners. We used to meet up and play bridge, but it was mostly to drink. I'll never understand how he never showed obvious signs of drink because he must have been an alcoholic. His second wife, Penny, certainly did. She died of cirrhosis of the liver. It was very sad actually because she was a lovely lady.

She phoned me one time to ask for help, "Jean, can you help me on the alcohol scene?"

"Yes, of course," I said. "I'll make an enquiry and let you know what I've arranged."

But when I arranged it, she didn't go and just went on drinking. She was actually a distant cousin. She absolutely adored her husband but was beginning to see that he was having affairs. She couldn't believe it at first. She had left her husband for him.

Rick and I really wanted to believe that our move was an amazing opportunity for a fresh start, but it wasn't. In the Midlands, Rick was a big cog in a small wheel but down south he was a small cog in a big wheel. He had become used to the status and culture we'd lived in up north where all the men knew each other and had this little club where they egged each other on to work harder and harder.

As life went on and Rick gathered more responsibilities, he became quite a pessimistic character. Rick had maintained his whole sense of identity from being at Esso. That's where he existed and where he got his fulfilment. Obviously, he adored his girls and was so proud of them, but he loved his work. And, in 1981, he had a breakdown and decided – and I can hardly bring myself to write it – that he wanted us to run our own petrol garage in south Croydon. It was the most terrible experience of my life. I had a nice job at the local hospital, and I was happy. But Rick wanted me at the garage with him. He wanted to prove to Esso that he could make money without being in head office. But of course, he couldn't, bless him.

I had no sense of self then. No sense of self at all. I just did what he wanted. And it was hell. I think I was going through the menopause at the time too, because I know I got terribly jealous about a woman he employed but it was irrational when I look back now. We had drive-offs and all the hassles that go with owning a garage. Rick employed a manager but couldn't let go and even with the manager there, he remained on site most of the time. I think he was just so addicted to being needed by the big oil company; he couldn't not do it. He was drinking very heavily at that time.

I was supposed to be doing the book-keeping. It's not in my nature to be a bookkeeper, so it was stressful. I was supposed to buying stuff for the shop, which I did. I went over to a big warehouse in Orpington and stocked up. Initially that was quite fun; like playing shop. I was very excited that it all went out very quickly and then I realized I hadn't been charging anyone VAT. No wonder we had such a shop full of happy customers!

We had the garage for two years. I can't think why we stopped. I think we were losing money but couldn't work out how. In the end Rick thought enough was enough. Alcohol played such a big part. I remember going to the supermarket and looking at people and wondering, do they have a hangover? In the evening, Rick would pour out Scotches and offer me one and I'd think, if only he'd offer me his company instead. But it made him feel better if I was keeping him company. Why didn't I say no? No voice!

Kate wasn't living with us when Rick's drinking really began to escalate. He never knew when to stop. There was a group of six of us who drank to excess when we were living in Sutton Coldfield, most of whom were in denial. When, some years later, I mentioned to one of the women that Rick was an alcoholic she said, "Oh don't be ridiculous!" Her husband was too.

Most people knew when to stop drinking but my darling husband didn't. He didn't want to lose that feeling, which is typical of an alcoholic. I was drinking too much too, but I knew when to stop. That was the difference.

* * *

In the summer of 1982, I turned 50. And my surprise birthday present was a trip in a hot air balloon over Kent. This was something I wanted to do, especially since I'd seen them from our garden silently gliding through the air.

On the day, we received a call to say there was some uncertainty about the flight due to the wind, but to go anyway. Rick, Kate and I arrived at the allotted field in Kent, to meet the pilot and a number of other ladies, all of whom were celebrating some event. The balloon was inflated, with ropes secured to a lorry. Eventually we were all told to get in the basket, which we did a little nervously, as there was still quite a gusty wind. Suddenly we shot up very quickly and we were off. Kate said afterwards that it was very funny to see the faces of these five ladies change from excitement to terror in one second flat.

All was well and we sailed into a new world of silence and calm. I had so many questions I was going to ask, but actually nobody wanted to speak as we floated over farms, cattle, horses, and fields. It was a joy. As we prepared to land, I think the wind was making it difficult as the pilot attempted one landing, but then changed his mind. We eventually came down in a large private estate owned by an Arab of note. No sooner had we landed than security men appeared with guns and dogs. Very funny really as it was unlikely that five very nervous ladies in a balloon were going to be a threat. We were hastily escorted off the grounds and through large security gates, where of course the lorry arrived to pick up balloon and pilot.

Rick and Kate had been dashing round the country lanes trying to trace the balloon, which was fun. I believe we all ended up in a pub for a glass of champagne. It was an amazing experience. We laughed and talked about it for a long time.

* * *

After the garage, Rick worked for an estate agent in Bromley. Jules was already working there, and Rick really enjoyed it. He was there for five years, until he retired. Then he and I bought a camper van, which we called Ginty – short for gin & tonic and we went round Europe for three months. The girls were off travelling themselves. We were such typical middle-class English people when we set off. We were uptight and terrified of everything. But by the time we got home, we didn't care what we looked like, and we talked to anybody and everybody. It was so refreshing. We thought we would never go back to suburbia again but of course we did. But it was a lovely experience to just get the freedom of responsibility. That's what it was – for both of us.

When we set off, we couldn't understand why lots of people were waving and cheering as they passed us. When we got down to Dover, we realised Sarah had tied a sign on the back of the van that said Just Married! It was a little bit like a honeymoon. It was a good time for our marriage. We were rather like a brother and sister in some ways, but it didn't matter to us. Or it might have mattered to Rick, I don't know. We didn't talk about that. We didn't talk about a lot of things. Couples didn't in those days.

We drank on the trip, of course, but I was drinking much less. Rick's drinking became intolerable when we were home. Every Monday he'd say, "I'm so sorry. I won't drink again."

One morning I left a note by the kettle saying I'd had it. When I came back, I told Rick that I wasn't going on any further unless he controlled his drinking. Remarkably and to his credit, he went to the doctor and the doctor suggested he record his drinks so that he only had one or two a night. And it worked for him.

CHAPTER THIRTEEN

"Our therapists have asked us if we realise that we've both been abused for years — sexually, financially, alcoholically and emotionally?"

In the mid-80s, when I was in my mid-50s, the tectonic plates of life cracked and broke open. I was going to learn that not only were times changing and that young people did speak out about their feelings, but that I was going to learn to do the same and experience the transformation of a lifetime. Or of this lifetime, anyway.

The girls had embarked on various travels and adventures, going across Europe on long train journeys and to Australia. Sarah had completed a children's nursery nurse course at Tunbridge Wells College. Then she did Montessori training in London. And after that, Doug's son Graham, asked her to go and be the nanny to his two children in Los Angeles.

While Sarah was in Los Angeles being a nanny, she became interested in some self-development seminars that Graham was attending and eventually started having therapy. Jules was also in America by this time, and by coincidence also started having therapy. It was much more popular in the States than in Europe at the time. They chatted, of course, and shared what they'd been speaking about with their therapists. Then they realized that they had both been unearthing their own, and family secrets.

They told me that whenever certain family members were in our company, they had been abusing them. Sarah and Julie also spoke about their Dad's drinking and said he was emotionally manipulative. Jules had a really hard time because although Rick adored her, he always said he could see his faults in her and he was always very hard on her. I don't think there was financial abuse, so I can't comment on that.

I was rocked to my core. At the time, I was working at the Institute of Cancer Research as a medical interviewer and I broke down in the office and told my colleagues, "My girls are accusing my husband and I of abusing them and not protecting them." One of my colleagues came to me with literature on False Memory Syndrome.

For Rick and me, it was like being hit with a sledgehammer. We had moved to Kemsing, a village in Kent, in 1984 and were enjoying living there, especially as most of the couples living in our cul-de-sac were our age and had similar interests to us. What we heard from our girls, who were felt so far away emotionally now as well as physically, sent us into a state of shock, confusion, pain, hurt, bewilderment, and loss, and anger – especially on Rick's part.

So, what did Rick and I do? We did what my family had always done when things became painful. We had a luncheon party, for all our new neighbours. Well, it was something we knew how to do, and it was familiar and a huge distraction to what was happening to our immediate family. We arranged for eight people to sit round our dining room table in one room, then another six or eight sat round the garden table in the sitting room. Large, tasty casseroles and dishes of mixed vegetables were served on both tables with red and white wine. After the main course we asked all the men to change rooms for the desserts. I don't know what desserts were offered but I do know it all proved a great distraction for us, for a short while anyway.

It was a lot of work, but everyone enjoyed themselves. As the guests were leaving, one of them said to me, "You've obviously done this before!" Which we had, but the next day we still had to endure the intense confusion we both felt as far as our family situation was concerned. We didn't know what Jules and Sarah were talking about. We had phone calls that went on and on. I didn't know how to deal with it.

That said, I believed them. Absolutely and without question. And immediately that caused a huge rift. I was totally on my own; Kate wasn't talking to me because I'd sided with the girls, in her opinion. My daughters are all intelligent women, and they all had their different approaches. It was heart-breaking – a mother's worst nightmare to see her children fall out so badly. Somebody had told me, years beforehand, that sometimes this sort of break-up between siblings, such as between Kate and Sarah and Julie, can take 10-12 years to heal. I really thought that I would go mad waiting for a reconciliation. I was scared witless and couldn't see an answer. And Rick wasn't talking to me either, just going around telling everybody, "You'll never believe what the girls have done. They've accused us of this, this and this."

Many family members cut me out too. They completely ostracized me because it looked like I was going against them. But I wasn't. I just wanted to help my daughters get through what they were going through. What else could I do? I had no choice but to keep going for the wellbeing of all my daughters. I was like a lioness with my cubs. I would have murdered someone to find out what was going on.

I call those years my wilderness years because I had nobody on my side or supporting me. I wanted everyone to go into therapy; I was told that the only way families heal with this is by all going to therapy but of course that didn't happen. At one stage, I was given even more devastating advice that it could take a family 10 years to heal from this kind of revelation and I thought I would simply not be able to live in the pain and turmoil for a decade.

I was trying to understand where the girls were coming from and what they were going through. Within a very short while of everything being revealed, Sarah wanted me to go over and speak to her therapist. I knew enough to know, at that time, that this was important for her healing. Sarah needed to hear from me that everything she was saying was true, in front of her therapist. So, without hesitating, I went. Apparently, my agreement that such things had happened was the best thing I could have said because I was validating Sarah – essential for abuse survivors and victims.

It was though seeing Sarah's therapist that I realised the impact on my girls. All this had happened under my nose and now I was finally seeing how wrong it was. I saw it in myself: my lack of boundaries, my lack of confidence, how I didn't think I could have an opinion on anything, how I didn't give myself permission to say no, or to question things. It was as if someone was lifting a mask from my eyes.

Stories came out of the woodwork then from some members of the family on a variety of subjects. The dam had truly been opened by Jules and Sarah.

Their therapists said this was very common in families. Not that this was healing to begin with. The girls were absolutely furious with Rick and me.

Above, me
off to school,
1937; right,
Mother,
Father and
little Bill,
June 1950

Shirl, Bill and me on beach spring, 1939, and at, right,
Seniors Farm, Semley, 1940

Both sets of grandparents: my paternal
grandfather, left; my maternal grandmother,
second right, who were brother and sister

Kate and Ellen with Kate's 100th birthday
cake

Top, Rick's memorial bench on the nature reserve in Kemsing; bottom, Blossom at campsite in Sevenoaks

Top, swimming
with dolphins
at San Diego
Zoo in May
2002; right, the
day of my 80th
birthday
standing in
front of some
of my artwork

My healing aids and accreditation

The flower arrangement inspired by Beethoven's Pastoral that was designed for the church in Kemsing. My friend, Elaine, helped a great deal (*see Chapter Eighteen*). Clockwise from top left, the images depict: Awakening of cheerful feelings; scene by the brook; shepherd's song; thunderstorm; and (*centre*) merry gathering of country folk

My sister Shirl with her children, around 1973

With my grandchildren Ellen, Lilia, Annabel and James, in July 2012

My dear husband, Rick

CHAPTER FOURTEEN

There was nothing for me to do but to go into therapy. I had also received the terrible news that a relative who I loved dearly had been diagnosed with HIV. I saw my GP who arranged for six weeks of counselling. But I was told I needed long-term therapy, so I continued privately for another 18 months, then went into group therapy for about six or seven years.

To say that therapy was a new experience for me was an understatement. I had never shared my feelings, or even acknowledged that I had feelings before. Not on any subject. I went in desperation. I was terrified and certainly didn't take to therapy like a duck to water. I felt as if I was existing on some strange, new planet. Along the way I learned how to best support the girls with what they had been through and were going through. But I had no support and was deeply lonely. I couldn't talk to Rick, or my friends or Kate.

I had always known that something untoward was going on in my family but looking deeply into what had occurred was excruciating. And it was during my therapy that I realised that I too, had been a victim of sexual abuse by various members of my family. It was as if the ground had been taken from under my feet. I had no idea that one's soul could hurt.

I didn't really understand the effect of it on me, at the time, how I had been shaped by my environment. My therapist had a tea towel. Twenty-four examples of how children are abused were listed on it. It might sound daft, but I learned a lot from that tea towel. That's probably why it was there. Some of the situations depicted were quite minor it seemed to me, but they were considered abuse.

It also slowly dawned on me that my mother and sister had been abused too. It was all so sick. There was my mother's father, Grandpa Johnson and later, a particular uncle did turn up in places where he knew my mother would be. He also went to Australia to visit Shirl. Once when I was out there visiting her, flowers arrived from him. She put them straight in the bin. I'll never know exactly what happened, but I believe it's obvious. Almost everyone had been a victim and it had gone on for generations. My father didn't molest my sister and I, but there were his inappropriate relationships with the maids, which my poor mother tolerated – again very common for victims and survivors of abuse.

My girls and I were now discovering the damage that sexual abuse wreaks on a woman's soul. Most of the women in my family had no sense of self or they wouldn't have put up with what they put up with. It seems likely that my mother's desperate trying to help others was likely a symptom of the low self-esteem that results from childhood abuse. When I think about it now, I can see that my mother was a courageous woman. She organised everybody all of the time. My take is that she didn't show outward signs that she had academic qualities as she was too busy trying to save the world. But her mind was quick and accurate. She would have made a wonderful nurse. She was efficient, fast, enthusiastic and a good delegator. As part of it all, I came to understand my mother much better. I miss her more now than I think I ever had done. I think since I've learnt more, understood more.

Even with the family abusers, I understand why they were as they were. But it would be years before that kind of insight developed.

As part of their therapy, the girls drew a family tree and marked on it who had been abused in some way. It's interesting to ask the question of how they knew that my mother and sister had been abused because they were aware of this even before I acknowledged my own abuse. But an experienced therapist would have seen that for my mother to have not protested against my being abused, she would have thought it was fairly normal. There's usually only one reason for that. She would not think that behaviour was normal unless she had experienced it herself.

As furious as they were, Jules and Sarah were helpful and supportive in helping me find the appropriate therapist, suggesting that when I attended first meeting of a potential therapist, I ask the right questions such as: how long have they been practicing, what licenses and qualification they have, their fees, whether they have had clients with similar circumstances to my own and if they have their own supervision. The girls' continued supporting me by sending me things like Native American Animal cards. I was given a set of Runes which Jules had made for everyone who attended her wedding, and a set of Affirmation Cards which are popular for someone starting therapy. They gave me advice about helpful books to read.

I ended up choosing a therapist from the local AA book. I chose her as she had so many qualifications to her name, and the moment I walked in I knew it was the right one. I was very nervous starting not knowing what I was letting myself in to. The most important thing, I would discover, is to gradually feel a deep trust for the therapist.

Jules was in L.A. and wouldn't see me for a number of years. I had to accept that, trusting that it would eventually change. And it did. I went to USA to join Jules and Sar in a workshop run in Yosemite National Park by their therapist. This proved to be a very profound experience in the renewal of our relationships. Later, Jules also asked me to go over when her husband went to prison. I didn't need to be asked twice and I was on the next flight. It was a breakthrough for us. I stayed for 10 days and on the 10th day, she was in the bath, and she told me, "I'm fine now, you can go."

"I know," I said. I felt it too.

But at first, the girls were angry, understandably, and they wanted and needed me to understand and acknowledge what they were saying. Rick never did. He never acknowledged what they had experienced. He couldn't bear to think that he hadn't protected them. He didn't realise there was anything to protect them from.

My parents lived a very fast, chaotic world which when I was young, I found scary in many ways. I'm now aware that Rick and I created the same situation for our girls, thinking it was the way to live. I eventually discussed this with my daughters, and they were definitely affected by it. Kate remembers walking into our pantry and seeing Rick kissing someone else. "I'm just thanking Uncle Rick for a lovely party," the woman told her. No wonder they all went travelling in an attempt to put that boundary in place.

I recently told Sarah that I'd had a terrible dream

where I was in the chaos we used to live in, in the Midlands. All these people coming and going. It was exactly like it was when a friend of ours found a sign that said: Coaches welcome. Bed and breakfast. He put it outside our house. That summed it up. All my girls recall it as a terrible time. I didn't know how to do it differently.

I saw my therapist weekly and don't remember much in detail except that the trust did develop. And eventually, she said, "Why don't you train to become a therapist yourself?" I don't think she saw potential in me necessarily. It was just that when you're in training, you have to be in therapy, and she knew that I would just learn more therapeutically. I was finding the whole subject so interesting and life changing. I did learn so much more. I wish I'd done it years earlier. But I wasn't meant to so there we go.

During my therapy training, I continued as a medical interviewer, which I had been doing at the Royal Marsden with breast cancer patients – interviewing ladies who had had the disease, seeking potential causes. I later began covering Kent interviewing parents of children with cancer, looking for the causes of that. These were case-control studies, so with the children, we also interviewed the parents of children who were the same age and didn't have cancer and compared them. It was a nice job for me to have at that time; I wasn't in an office, I was driving around with my own thoughts and my own awareness, thinking about behaviour and why people behave the way they do. I often used to take my tape recorder and talk into it. I was dealing with my daughters' recoveries as well as my own. It's a heavy burden as a mother.

I started my training in 1997. There were usually about a dozen of us that term. That was challenging especially as I was by far the eldest and anyone who had issues with their mother would take it out on me. To start with I would burst into tears, but then I learned to hold my ground and retaliate appropriately. This was a huge lesson for me as gradually started doing this at home too. I found it was okay and it worked.

It was like being slowly born again only this time in to a safe, respectful and loving world. I learnt about enmeshed relationships and how to deal with them. The revelations and enlightenments kept coming – some small, some large. I had new and healthy awareness, constantly realising why I or someone else did this or that.

One autumn at the beginning of a new term, I noticed the son of a social friend of mine was starting with me. This was quite a shock as I had kept my therapy life and social life very separate. I thought this was probably a sign to bring both lives together, which is what I did. Of course, the young man and I had to do a lot of work around boundaries and confidentiality. He went on to become a very successful therapist.

As part of my training I was required to be in supervision with a practicing qualified therapist. I was lucky to go to a vicar who ran a therapy group for adults with learning difficulties. I was apprehensive before I started but, again, I learned so much and even ran the group when the vicar was away.

I was in supervision for about a year and after four years of training, I was required to write a 3,000-word essay on a chosen subject, in order to achieve my Diploma in Personal Psychotherapy, achieving this in 2004. I wrote on the subject of Ego States, learning about how we can relate to each healthily and respectfully.

I was also in group therapy for just over a year meeting once and sometimes twice a week – 80 times in all. I'm not sure how it came about but my therapist suggested it. I seem to remember I only knew one or two other members in the group. There were between six and eight of us. Initially we spent our time together getting to know each other as we shared our individual stories. Then gradually over the weeks, as we grew to trust each other, more profound issues were discussed. One of the new reactions I learned was to not react physically if someone was upset and crying. Just to support them in their discomfort but to not try to make them better. This allows one to really move through the pain. Giving someone that minute or two, rather than a hug is healthy, especially when one usually wants to make it better for your own comfort.

I spent most of my time for a number of weeks talking about the total collapse of my own family. Accusations, pain, anger, confusion disbelief and bewilderment, I shared it all. Until, after a number of weeks of doing this, one of the group said to me, "Jean, I am so bored with hearing all about your family, and who is talking to who and who is not. I want to hear about you, what makes you laugh or cry, what music you like? Do you like animals for example?"

I was absolutely amazed to be spoken to like this. I felt cross, infuriated, embarrassed and much more. Then of course the rest of the group were asked what they thought, and they all felt the same.

During the half hour drive home in the dark I thought, I didn't know there was a me and I just didn't know where to start. The words of that woman were such a gift.

CHAPTER FIFTEEN

I've decided to share, in my memoir, one of the assaults I was objected to that I've never spoken of before – you can turn the page if you don't want to know. I just want to get it out there. It happened one evening when I was in my 20s, I think, and in an uncle's car, sat between him (he was driving) and his wife. Unknown to me, he undid his trousers and then surreptitiously took my hand and placed it round his naked penis.

And what did I do? Nothing. I froze as fear, anger and embarrassment washed over me to the point where I think I completely disassociated. Even remembering the incident traumatises me and I feel so sad that I did nothing. That uncle had done many other things to me over the years, but nothing as blatant and horrifying as that. I understand now that I cannot blame myself for freezing. It's a very common response, akin to playing dead and replicated all across the animal world when an attack is under way, and you cannot fight or flee. Your body chooses the response, not you.

On another occasion, a few months after my sister died, I felt I needed to get away. I didn't want to visit anyone who had been really close to Shirl, so I phoned a dear aunt, who I had had always liked and admired, and I chose a weekend when I knew her husband was sailing.

She gave me everything I was requiring, peace and emotional space – as she spent all day gardening. I had lovely hot baths using all the lovely smelly things she put out for me, and after three days I felt peaceful again. That was until one evening when her husband phoned. When he heard I was staying there, he came straight home. I should have left then but I didn't. That night he came to my room and tried to have sex with me. Again, I froze out of sadness, embarrassment and a feeling of being worthless of anything better and he left the room.

I know this will be difficult reading for many, but the shame is not mine to carry, and I no longer want to be burdened with carrying the secrets of the past.

* * *

In some ways, discovering and remembering all the things that had happened was a hallelujah moment. I thought everything was normal. I was told. "You mustn't complain about it. He doesn't mean anything, darling. That's how he is. Don't take any notice."

Even after I was married, I tried to avoid being in a room with those uncles. One of them had abused my girls in the same way he abused me. He was inappropriate with them. They all thought, which is common (and which I thought too) that he liked them. He made people feel special. "Look everyone, he's dancing with me! And he thinks I'm great company."

I grew up thinking promiscuity in our family was the norm. I grew up thinking it was okay to flirt and to dance inappropriately. But being promiscuous is one thing, and it's fine between consenting adults. But nobody was consenting to this. There were abusers in our midst, they held the power, and many of the people who should have been telling them to cut it out – like my parents – propped them and told me it was all fine and nothing to worry about. And I perpetuated this. I didn't allow the girls to be abused, but I didn't protect them from it either. I saw that man dancing with Julie inappropriately and it didn't cross my mind to say, "Cut that out now." I have another friend about my age, and she saw him dancing with her daughter inappropriately and she went straight up and said something. Obviously, she hadn't had the same experiences as me and knew this was wrong.

It was a long time before I felt believed by many people. But not too long ago, I was at a funeral and speaking to my cousin Paul who I've always had an affinity with. "I'm writing a book," I told him," and I want to say that I came from an abusive, dysfunctional south London family. But I don't know if I can use that word – abusive."

"Well, thank goodness someone has finally said it!" Paul said. And I just wept. I felt so free and vindicated. People had known! It had all been swept under the carpet, but people had known.

The worst offender died before Jules and Sarah spoke out. But the other person, who hadn't enacted any physical abuse – more sexual innuendo and inappropriate comments was still alive. Jules said she found this behaviour very confusing and of course, it would have added to the general atmosphere of acceptance that certain things were okay when they were not. Jules and Sarah did not want to go to the police.

Recently, Kate sent me a photograph of a party she had been to that one of the perpetrators had attended. I hadn't gone because I was in the midst of my therapy and was completely terrified of seeing him. Just seeing that photo was a reminder of how deeply I was affected by everything.

The event was Maida's and her husband's Golden Wedding. I was incapable of going as I was in the deepest and most painful and frightening period of my personal healing journey. My decision caused great upset in my own family as Kate and Jonathan went without Rick and I, which was embarrassing for them, and I received many phone calls telling me I had made Maida cry over my decision. It feels extraordinary now to remember just how fearful I felt at that time.

Rick and I invited Maida and Freddie to come for a private celebratory lunch. I was delighted that they graciously accepted. After lunch Maida and I were on our own in my bedroom and she told me she had been abused by two of her brothers. I don't think for a moment she ever understood the effects of that or the work my girls and I were going through to heal.

And it wasn't just one brother. My father's brother was the one I always safe with and yet, during my therapy, he came to stay at our home and when I asked him, "Did you have a nice sleep last night?" He replied, "Yes. I woke up and had an erection just thinking about you."

I did nothing for about an hour. And then I was able – with my new voice – to say, "You know, what you said just now was totally inappropriate and upset me."

He said, "I'm sorry. I shouldn't have said that."

He stayed with us for another couple of days, which is remarkable. And then I know he would have driven home all confused asking himself what the matter is with me. That's how the family responded:

"What's the matter with Julie and Sarah? They've gone a bit silly."

* * *

With Rick so furious, it was fortunate that I was earning enough to go to America without asking for money. He was devastated and wouldn't try to understand what was going on.

"You've made this choice not to look at it," I told him.

I think he knew something was going on. Of course, he did. He was at the parties and saw it going on. But he didn't have the background or the personality, he didn't have what people have today, to step in and say, "Cut that out." He just didn't get it.

Before I went into therapy, a very precious niece came to me sobbing one day and said, "I thought Doug loved me."

"He does," I said.

"He just kissed me goodbye and rubbed himself all up against me though," she continued.

"Oh darling, that's what he's like," I said, completely belittling what she'd been through.

Many years later I realized this was such an awful thing to say so I went to see her, to apologise. "I do apologise for saying that," I said. "I always want what's absolutely best for you and my saying that to you wasn't right."

I don't think I would ever have found my voice if it hadn't been for the work Jules and Sar did, the books they suggested I read. It has been an absolute gift to have had two daughters on their own similar journey of self-discovery. Observing the girls' pain was much worse than what I was going through. But there was only so much I could do. They've had to do their own journey. We're so proud of each other because it has been hard and very lonely. I changed as a human being, as a woman.

I learned an enormous amount during my own years in therapy. I remember saying to my therapist once, "I think if I cry, I won't be able to stop."

She replied very calmly, "You will only cry a maximum of 10 minutes to start with."

But through all the turmoil, I've found my voice. As a woman in my family, you didn't have a voice. I remember small things that happened when I started to realise I could say what was on my mind. I think the first was when I publicly said I didn't drink alcohol anymore. This was in 1998 around the time of mine and Rick's ruby wedding anniversary. That cause quite a kerfuffle as it makes people question their own drinking habits. When I turned up with my alcohol-free wine to a party, they'd announce, "Where's Jean's special bottle?" At one party I went to, someone offered me a drink and when I said I didn't drink, he said, "Gosh, how boring you must be!" To be fair to him, Rick was very accepting.

Another incident would occur when I was driving somewhere with my husband and as usual, he was being critical about my driving. Instead of accepting it, I said, "If you don't like it, do you want to get out?"

And when we went out for a meal, I would tell Rick, "If you have more than two drinks, I will get a taxi home." There were so many little examples of ways in which I developed a new persona. It was terrifying, but empowering. I felt so brave. Gradually, gradually I did this more often – how good that felt. Finding my voice was like finding a precious new muscle, and the more I used it, the stronger I could feel it becoming.

CHAPTER SIXTEEN

Finally, I was learning to feel things from the effect and injustice and pain of the abuse to the heartbreak of Bill and Shirl, the loss of my parents and the way in which Rick and I had raised our girls. For years I wondered why we felt distant from our friends. But really, they felt distant from us – because we were a family out of control. Since we were out of touch with our feelings, how could we be in touch with other people's?

Then, during my therapy training it was suggested we write about someone we'd lost so I wrote about Bill and what it was like for me when he was ill.

* * *

I wrote this for Bill, as part of my therapy.

"I'm going to start by writing how it was for me when you died, Bill.

"I really hadn't spent a lot of time with you at all in our time on this earth. So, you were taken ill. I really don't even remember being told what was going on. It all seems somewhat unreal, like remembering a very old film. There was a lot of coming and going of visitors, family members, doctors, nurses etc. I remember you being a very happy, brave little boy, but I just felt very remote.

"Do you know this was a very lonely time for me?

"And you became more and more unwell. I can remember you sitting in your wheelchair in the garden that summer, supposedly watering he garden with the hose, but you kept spraying Shirley and me. We had fun and laughed together.

"I remember midnight feasts we used to have when you were well. And bless you, you were so young that Shirley and I had a job keeping you awake.

"I remember you going off to that first school Carn Brae. You looked so smart in your yellow cap and grey blazer trimmed with yellow. All the time I felt very much the big sister.

"I remember us all being in the shelter in the cellar during the war, and you did have a job going to sleep. But do you know I don't remember playing with you or reading to you? I suppose I must have done at some time, but I can't remember.

"And so, you died on July 11, 1950, age 11 at 5.30am.

"And so, our home fell apart.

"There was a very large funeral. No tears – must be strong.

"I don't feel I ever said goodbye and I want to do that now some 50 something years later.

"I feel angry with you for dying. It is hard for me to write that because you were always my little brother and

118

in life, I don't think I would have ever got angry with you about anything. I was actually very jealous of you because you were so obviously the favourite child and totally idealised, almost worshipped. Of course, you didn't realise that, but many did.

"Anyway, our home became a very, very sad place for a long time after you died. In some ways I can hardly bring myself to write this but after you died, I thought now, maybe someone will see me. But no one ever really did. I can't honestly say I missed you initially. Life had been so awful that in some ways it was almost a relief that it was all over,

"But of course, it never was.

"This is a letter I wrote to you some time ago.

Dear Billy,

This feels so strange, as I've known you for so, so long and yet I feel I've only just met you. I remember you as a very nice, brave, thoughtful, fun-loving little boy. But I just didn't know you as you didn't know me. In fact, none of us knew anything about the other. We really weren't around each other much. You were always with Mum, and it was although you lived in another world to me. I guess it was as it was meant to be, but just today I suddenly feel so sad that we hadn't been closer and grown up together. I just feel like saying over and over again today out loud: "I'VE HAD A BROTHER. I'VE HAD A BROTHER. Everyone listen! I've had a brother and his name was Bill. He was my brother. He was my brother."

"I do wish you were still with me. I wonder, would we have been friends? I like to think we would."

* * *

I also wrote in depth about Shirley.

March 6, 2002.

Well I can't put this off any longer. It has been with me a lot recently, but of course it has been with me always.

What is it? It is the feeling of outrage, anger, fury, sadness, loneliness, isolation, abandonment etc.

I know at some level I felt this when other members of my family died. No one took care of my needs or asked how I was feeling or even spent time with me. Everyone was so busy being sad on their own. Or when we were all together, we were expected to all be brave for each other. Then I was told how wonderful I was, how I was holding everyone together.

I was told I was, "managing very well". But now I realise there was part of me screaming out to be loved, cared for and heard. I didn't want to, "get on" "get back to school" or "get back to normal", whatever that was. I wanted someone to know I was scared and frightened and lonely and tired of being strong.

I wanted to be told the truth too, and not just wonder what was happening or what people, doctors, specialists, nurses were thinking. I really wanted to cry and be told that I was all right.

I really found it hard to be brave all the time.

The footsteps were there in my hour of need,
Beside me all the way

To the beach I had gone, for the peace, oh the peace
At the end of that terrible day
After the pain and sorrow of a troubled life
My Shirl was called beyond
The laughter, the tears and the rows we had shared
All now ended...there was a very strong bond
As I strolled down the beach on the warm soft sand
And the spray of the sea in my face
The only sound was the gulls, swooping over my head
When suddenly my heart began to race
As I looked down at my feet now covered with sand
I saw two other footprints with mine
When I stopped, they stopped and when I moved, they
moved
Always with me and completely in time

What was happening here? My mind in a whirl
I look down again, at my now still feet
And there they were right next to mine
I could feel peace, just peace and more peace
Now sixteen years on since that very sad day
And there has been many a time
When trying to guide our girls and Shirl's children
I have felt her footsteps with mine.
It's a great solace to feel that peace is so near
And it has helped me many a time. Move than just
once
It has given me great comfort in times of need
Just to feel those footsteps with mine

My life has continued with family and love
But I'm surprised from time to time
That in the normal living of everyday life
I can still feel those footsteps with mine

I sat with my precious younger sister, Shirl, almost continuously for two days and two nights until she slowly passed away. We never spoke again. I had visited her in hospital two days earlier, she had her last chemotherapy injection and slipped into unconsciousness, from which she never recovered.

The nurses told me one's hearing is the last sense to operate before one passes away. So, I would tell Shirl when I was going for a walk, or for a newspaper or a snack or a wash. I didn't want to leave her as she had been so lonely and so very frightened and unhappy for so long.

We never had a really close relationship. We were the product of a very strict dysfunctional family who never really talked about anything. One just had to learn to how to survive on one's own – enjoying the good times and using whatever for the bad times.

My darling only, fun-loving, beautiful, crazy, sociable, kind, caring sister and I shared a unique sense of humour of fun and the ridiculous and we just had to look at each other to know what the other was thinking.

* * *

I found a note I'd written to Shirl. I'm not sure how it starts but it goes on to say:

"In fact, being so stoic when you and your family went to live in Sydney, I believe eventually lead to your illness and subsequent death.

"We were a totally unconscious family at that time, and had been for generations using drugs, alcohol, affairs and parties to survive, and we all thought we were having a wonderful time.

"Wow – crash, bang – the world came tumbling down when Jules and Sar went into therapy. This event really drew a big line under so much. There was then a very painful gap of many years, but gradually very slowly a new awareness took seed, and started to grow and grow and is still blooming stronger and stronger every day.

"I miss you and wish you were here with me, to observe the new healthy, awareness. But it wasn't to-be.

"Thank you for being my sister!"

CHAPTER SEVENTEEN

I thought it would be lovely if Rick went over to America on his own without me to see Jules and Sarah. He was reluctant but we had lunch one day with another friend of mine, who is a district nurse, and her husband. I said to her husband, "Tell me something. If you knew one of your daughters was unhappy and stressed in another country, would you go out there and see what the problem was?"

"Of course," he said.

When we got home, Rick said, "Maybe I will go." So, he went. They talked about all sorts of things. I don't even know what, but they were quite important things apparently. One of the things was my affair. They were all sat down to dinner, I gather, and asked him how he put up with that. I don't know how Rick answered.

As well as my therapy, having seen Sarah change as a result of the self-development seminars she was doing, I thought, I want some of this! So, I went and did it in London. She became more assertive. She was just generally happier. She was clear about what she wanted and what she didn't want; what she would put up with and wouldn't put up with. My husband wasn't too pleased of course when I did it but there you go.

It took years before I was able to say to the girls, "Just remember, when you were born, at some level, your soul chose to have me as your mother and dad as your father. Whatever you're learning in this lifetime, you're learning through me."

I like to believe that. I think it's helpful. They believe it too, so that's helpful for them as well.

Yesterday, Julie texted me to ask what time she was born, and I couldn't remember. What was significant was that I was able to joke and say, "Another failure added to the list!"

It took me years before I could joke about these things. For many years I wondered if I'd got anything right at all.

* * *

For some reason, one morning when I was writing this memoir, I woke up with the memory of the song sung by Bing Crosby and the Andrew Sisters, called Don't Fence me In. When I was in my late teens, Doug wanted to buy me the record because he knew

I liked it.

I really resonated with the words, "Oh, give me land lots of land and a starry sky above. But don't fence me in…"

I loved it because I so wanted to escape from the restrictions of living in my family – the relentless disciple of being taught manners, no lies, no fibs, no acknowledgement that I really existed, feeling I was a great disappointment to family by not being a boy. Continual criticism of everything. I completely lost who I was through fear of disapproval. "Can't you even make a custard without leaving lumps in it?"

The claustrophobic feeling of always feeling I was in the wrong.

The main feeling was one of fear.

CHAPTER EIGHTEEN

In the midst of all that was going on, in about 1990, Rick and I went to a Greek island to spend a week with a Dr Horace Dobbs who studied the spirit of dolphins. About 16 of us stayed in a rather primitive house up in the hills. Most of the other attendees were healers of some kind. I hadn't realised that would be the case, and I think Rick and I had one of the best holidays ever.

For me it was a joy to watch how Rick reacted to everyone especially as he just didn't have anything in common with any of them on a superficial level. It caused much amusement when after an alfresco dinner one evening he was heard to exclaim, "Doesn't anyone talk cricket?" But he was very popular with everyone and even participated in meditation and had a Reiki treatment.

On morning a boat had been hired and we all set out on a small coach to drive to the local harbour where we set sail in hope of seeing the dolphins, which to everyone's joy we did. While we were waiting for them to (hopefully) appear, I was intrigued to hear a lady who was a spiritual healer say, with her eyes closed, "They're here!" and then suddenly they were, swimming alongside us and swerving from side to side. It was truly a sight to behold. The next day we were asked to write a poem showing what effect the meeting of the dolphins had had on each of us. The poems were amazing and very moving.

I turned 60 in 1992 and with the girls abroad and relations slightly strained, Aunt Kath, some of the cousins and our neighbours came to a luncheon party, which we held in our garden. For the first time, Rick arranged for caterers to bring everything – food, china, cutlery and glasses – and then to take all the dirty things away. It was such a treat. I remember sitting in our sitting room and listening to all the activity in the kitchen. Music to my ears. The icing on the cake was that Sarah arrived as a surprise. It was a happy day and to my delight Rick surprised me by revealing that he had booked for he and I to go to Venice for three nights. It was somewhere I had always wanted to go. We had a hotel within walking distance of St Mark's Square and overlooking the water. Just perfect.

We walked a lot, exploring and tasting yummy things in little cafes. We went to one of the Murano islands to watch the beautiful glass ornaments being made and looked round an ancient church which had the most amazing ceramic floor.

One morning I asked Rick if he would like to get up really early and walk with me to St Mark's Square. He declined so I went on my own, and it was totally magical – completely empty, when the previous day it had been bustling with crowds. I was strolling around when a beautiful sound came from St Mark's Basilica where the choir were singing. The memory sends shivers up my spine even now.

Gradually the square started to wake up and I strolled back to the hotel to join Rick for breakfast. It was a very special three days in spite of Rick drinking a lot and sadly not feeling too well. I felt lonely as a result at times, but overall, I had a memorable birthday and felt very lucky.

*   *   *

As I waited for myself and my family to heal, life went on and in 1997, the members of the floral church group in Kemsing were asked to create an arrangement for the church. The arrangement had to depict a piece of music.

Without a great deal of thought I chose Beethoven's pastoral. Then I realised that I had no idea how to tackle the project and contacted a very creative friend called Elaine. She had lived in

Derbyshire and was familiar with how the village wells were decorated every year. With that in mind, we started pressing flowers of all kinds. Flowers from the garden, buttercups and daisies and wildflowers, in fact anything that was colourful, as well as rice and lentils. Many books in both houses were used to press our multitudes of flowers. Our camping table was erected in our sitting room and after weeks of flower pressing all the different colours were placed in separate piles. Eventually a design was created of the five movements of Beethoven's Pastoral.

Of course, it took many weeks, and if truth be told Elaine was definitely in charge. Amusingly, some evenings I would look at our work and perhaps move one or two flowers. The next time Elaine came and joined me she would re-do what I had changed with no comment. We laughed a lot about this later.

*   *   *

In September 2001, it was Rick's 70th birthday. We were certainly moving slowly towards reconciliation as a family and Jules, Sar, and one of Jules' stepdaughters came from the USA for the occasion. Before the actual day, we girls went to Paris by Eurostar for three days.

One morning when watching television in my room I saw what I thought was an old film being played, but suddenly I realised it was for real. The

Twin Towers in New York were under attack. I went to the girls' room and suggested they put television on. There was silence then tears. Their first thoughts were: what shall we do, where shall we go?

We went to The George Cinq Hotel where people had gathered to watch and listen to the commentators. It was interesting for me to hear all the girls say they wanted to go home. When I asked, "Where?" they all said, "America, of course," causing me to let out a big, silent sigh.

I seem to remember that after many phone calls we returned to Kent the next day. We managed to have a special day for Rick. He did so enjoy having his girls around.

My 70th birthday came next, at the same time as Sarah's graduation. It was June 2002, and Rick and I were invited to John F Kennedy University in San Francisco where Sarah had got her degree in Transpersonal Psychotherapy. Sarah found a delightful little house for Rick and me to stay in. The owners had taken a trip to Europe.

It was during Sarah's time at university that a tutor pointed out to Sarah that she had dyslexia and taught Sar how to adjust her learning. Sar has always called that tutor her educational midwife and it was such a wonderful celebration. Sarah had worked hard to work and study – financing herself completely – and after the graduation, we enjoyed a delightful dinner with close friends.

After leaving San Francisco, Rick and I flew to Los Angeles to spend some time with Jules in Venice, where she lived. We were really having a wonderful trip, but it wasn't finished as one evening Jules said to me, "We're leaving very early tomorrow morning to take you on a surprise birthday treat."

"But I haven't had my hair done," I said.

Jules smiled. "You won't need your hair done, Mum."

At the crack of dawn the next day we set off to goodness knows where and an hour and a half later, we drove into San Diego Zoo. I was very confused until I was given a certificate telling me I was a zoo attendant for a day ending with a swim with a dolphin – something I had always wanted to do. To say I was excited was an understatement. Sarah had flown down to LA to join us on this trip.

After a number of hours enjoying a tour of the zoo, I was taken to a little room where I was given a wet suit to wear. I was beside myself by this point. There was a short walk to the pool, then I went down some steps and got into the water with the dolphins. How magical was that! What has stayed with me especially, was to hear them chatting away under the water. I looked up and saw the family who were watching me having an extraordinary experience. After the obligatory photo hugging a dolphin, I left the water, got dressed and we all drove home. What an amazing joint 70th birthday present from them all.

Rick and I stayed for a few more days and then flew home.

CHAPTER NINETEEN

In the post-therapy years, Rick was unhappy due to being retired. He was also unwell. We had decided on a trip to India and spent ages planning it. But then he got a gall bladder problem. Now that's anger, that is – it manifests in the gall bladder. He had that operation and then he got Rheumatoid Arthritis, which was awful because he was in such pain.

The one night, we were asleep in bed and he woke me up, unable to breathe. He had all the symptoms of a heart attack. We called the GP who came immediately then told us to go to hospital the next morning. I always thought that was a strange thing for a GP to advise. When we got to the hospital, Rick needed a bypass and luckily, he was able to have it done privately and therefore very quickly.

Not long after that, we had to move because our money was running out and we didn't own our house. I found quite a nice little one locally, but it wasn't the standard Rick wanted. I don't say that unkindly – his pride wouldn't let him move into a house he didn't like. So, we didn't do anything except borrow more money on the house.

Then he went to the doctor with swollen glands, which turned out to be Hodgkin's Lymphoma. Rick had chemotherapy, which was awful. Then we moved to this horrible little house in Sevenoaks. I remember going in the garden and him telling me, "Next summer we won't be here," meaning that we would move.

When my husband was ill, he knew I'd changed as a result of therapy, and I asked him, "Do you prefer the new Jean or the old Jean?" He said, "I much prefer the new Jean." I didn't quite know what he meant by that. But by God I've changed as a woman! Hallelujah to that.

We were like two children trying to bring up three children. We both came from such dysfunctional families. I was very pleased he was an only child; I didn't want to marry into a big family, having had a big family. No thank you! He, having had no big family, wanted to marry into a big family. He didn't realise how dysfunctional they were. So, somehow, we got through it and, when I think back now, God knows how we did. I just don't know how we did, but actually we did love each other. We were, on reflection, two wounded people who loved each other in the only way we could.

We did our best with our beautiful girls and were delighted to see each of them find partners along the way. In the late 90s, Jules married Bill Dale in a traditional Native American Wedding at Zaca Lake California. I didn't have any kind of role as mother of the bride. Jules had her therapist there as her main support, which she regrets now, but it shows what shape our relationship was in. The marriage lasted ten years. It wasn't sad that the marriage didn't last, it was just the next step in Jules and Bill's individual journeys. In December 2002, Sarah and Shawn were married by a friend in the grounds of Grace Cathedral in San Francisco. Sarah has since told me she wouldn't have changed that for anything. They renewed their vows inside the cathedral in 2012. This poignant event was attended by close friends, Jules and me. Just inside the cathedral is a magnificent labyrinth round which everyone walked before attending the actual service held in one of the side chapels. It was a beautiful and very spiritual service. Afterwards, we had dinner is a cosy, intimate Italian restaurant. Jules and I left a little early as I had arrived from England only the previous day, so was a little weary.

Sadly without Rick present, Kate married Jonathan Tempest in August 2010. It was a beautiful weekend wedding celebration attended by close family, friends, and sisters, brother-in-law and nieces from California. The ceremony was conducted in the grounds of a hotel in the Lake District with their two children, James and Ellen, and Cousin Lilia, as page boy and bridesmaids. The weekend was enjoyable with fun pub lunches, rides in boats on the lake, beautiful walks and an extra enjoyable post wedding lunch at another hotel! We were spoiled with glorious weather – a uniquely lovely weekend.

*   *   *

Rick did have some happy times in Sevenoaks, but it eventually became obvious that he wasn't going to survive. But when we knew it was time to ensure the girls were there, they all came and that was a healing time for the three of them. That was when the three of them got on. It was just extraordinary. Kate had hardly spoken to her sisters in 10 years and there we were at this tiny, horrible little house in Sevenoaks, arranging hospital visits.

Jules says she got to know her father on his death bed. I think that's sort of true. She visited him in intensive care, and they had some amazing conversations.

In the end, the doctors explained that it would be best to take Rick off life support. Rick had all of his girls around him – he always felt better with all of his girls around him – and we were all together as he said goodbye to this world on December 3, 2003.

It was very unpleasant for Kate and I as there had

to be an inquest into Rick's death as the doctors admitted negligence. We had to wait 10 months for the inquest, which was held in Tunbridge Wells. It was difficult to hear that Rick had accidentally been given a child's dose of antibiotics.

When Rick died, there was a part of me which was relieved. I had been looking after him for so long. I know when he was first diagnosed, I burst into tears because it brought back memories of when my sister was diagnosed in Australia. And I know, and I do believe in all honesty, that his soul wanted to leave his body five years before it did. In today's society, medical science keeps bringing people back. Sometimes they don't want to come back. Even Jules in particular says her father was ready to go years before. It is true. I find that a bit of a help. It was meant to be.

After Rick's death, my therapist says that I was in denial for a long time. I think I was. I don't think I really grieved until years afterwards. I was left in this horrible little house with two cars that both broke down the week he died. I didn't have a car and I had to rent one. Then there was no money anywhere. I had to borrow money to pay for the funeral.

As a memorial for Rick, I bought a bench that was placed in Kemsing Down Nature Reserve, a place where Rick and I loved to walk. A memorial plaque reads: Beloved husband, father and grandfather.

Kate and I placed his ashes under the bench.

* * *

My wonder therapist Joanna had bought a campervan and it got me thinking. One day I asked her, "Do you think I should buy a campervan?" She knew how much money I didn't have but she said, "Yes," and that was it. With a small insurance Rick had taken out, and after many trips to see various vans, I finally found one that I liked that had one lady owner. I had done it – I had bought my camper van and off I went. That was what really saved the day. The joy of it was that nobody knew where I was and that seemed perfect to me.

I travelled locally and also took trips to the New Forest and Canterbury. But my main adventure was making my way around England, finding grandmothers and granddaughters to interview.

It was absolutely the best thing I could have done. I had to learn how to get water, gas and change the two batteries – one for the car and one for lighting. I shed tears, of course, when things went wrong once or twice, but I found Jean again.

* * *

On December 3, 2006, I wrote on the anniversary of Rick's passing:

"Well, here I am in Knowle Park with a flask of

coffee and a bar of Cadbury's choc. It is a sunny but windy day and I have been wondering how to acknowledge this day appropriately for me to feel at peace with.

I had a 30-minute meditation, then drove here in Blossom. I didn't feel like going up to the bench as I had originally planned as that sounded too hard, so decided this was the place where I wanted to write a few words on how it has felt since Ricky's Spirit left his body.

I miss you very much in so many ways, and I honestly believe my soul/spirit was meant to spend 45 years with your soul.

Our lives were exactly as they were meant to be. I sometimes think 'I should/ shouldn't have done that or said that etc etc etc,' but in thinking that it takes away the good things.

We both had very young spirits really, and I think at some level we both knew that but just didn't know what to do about it.

I so miss your spirit being with me, your quietness, your gentleness and your humour, which I sort of didn't honour. Quietness wasn't in my repertoire then as it is now, and oh how I celebrate that I have at last prioritised quietness.

I am to a certain extent enjoying my time with just me in a way I don't think we could have together in our 47 years. It just wasn't meant to be.

We had to face quite a number of health challenges

in those last few years, didn't we? It was hard but we made it didn't we.

And right to the end your soul/spirit decided not to leave until you had all your family together with you. You certainly showed them the courage you possessed at that terrible time, and even at that time you had some special time with them.

St Mary's Church was totally full to capacity with love and acknowledgement of the uniquely wonderful man you were on this earth at that time.

I know at that time I had a quick wish that I could always have been the women I was at that time.

I was going to tell you about your precious daughters and grandchildren, but you know all about their lives don't you.

I know your spirit is very much alive in all of us, and for that I am so grateful.

I can physically feel great love in my heart

The deer are right in front of Blossom and I'm now going to walk round the house.

I'm so pleased I have done this today.

I'm going to surround myself in white healing light as I walk."

*   *   *

In June 2009, I had a vivid dream about Rick. I still remember the dream to this day, and it brings with it such sadness. I dreamt I was running around

Somerville Road (our home in Sutton Coldfield) looking for him. I ran from room to room, which all looked exactly as they were when we lived there – same furniture, pictures, even the girls' rooms were all the same. They were there and I said to them, "We really must throw out all this stuff now mustn't we, as we won't need it anymore."

I kept running round calling Rick but just couldn't find him. I got into our bed but realised I hadn't slept there the previous evening, but someone had. Rick walked in and said he wasn't going to sleep there. When I asked him why he said, "I sleep somewhere else now." I was so looking forward to having my arm round him, but he walked out. I was very sad and puzzled.

Looking back, I think about my intimate relationship with my husband, which of course was affected by my history, but also by realising that my precious husband had issues around this subject also. With his parents in India, he attended boarding school and told me a little of the bullying that went on there, which I know upset him. Who knows what else happened? I do know that our relationship never had an intimacy as I know exists today and is seen as normal. I never really experienced this, and I certainly never saw this in my family as a child. I realise that we both had issues around intimacy as we had never seen it or experienced it. I guess this was another reason for his drinking, and mine too, until I stopped. It just helped to hide something big that was missing in our lives.

Rick once told me he wanted to have the words: "I'm sorry," engraved on his headstone, directed at his parents, since he felt he had let them down by failing at school, then failing to become an officer in the army and finally by failing his accountancy finals. Is it any wonder he worked so hard to try and prove himself, and drank to mask his feelings of failure? It's so sad.

CHAPTER TWENTY

Back at home after my travels with Blossom, it was no longer an option to stay in Sevenoaks. I realised I wasn't the same person, not only because of the work I'd done through therapy, but because I was on my own. Every coffee shop I went into and every walk I went on, Rick was there, and I missed him hugely.

I didn't know where to go. I always thought I'd go to the coast. But with Kate in Oxford and the others in America, it was the obvious thing to do to move to Poffley End into a house beside Kate. She was quite happy about it.

My grandchildren came quite late in life for me because both Kate and Sarah were much older parents than I was. Kate's eldest, James, will be 21 in November 2021. He was two when Rick died. Rick absolutely adored him.

Ellen was born in November 2002. Sarah had Lilia the following year, then Annabelle.

I have loved being a grandmother. It opens up a part of your heart you didn't even know you had and that's the truth of it. I have also been able do some things differently to how I did them with the girls.

In April 2012, Jules asked me how I wanted to celebrate my 80th birthday. I suggested having a special tea, maybe at Blenheim Palace. This idea was shot down, so Kate and I set off on a mission to find a perfect place where we could host a luncheon for about 30 people. After much searching, we found that a nearby pub had recently had an extension built and could cater for up to 50 guests, and after deliberating, we booked it.

Then the difficult task of who to invite began. Family, friends and neighbours were chosen. At one point, Kate said to me, "You can't ask that one if you don't ask this one." I worried about it for days, but then I told her, "Do you know what? When you're 80 you actually can." So that's what I did.

Jules' suggestion was that I invite everyone who had supported me along the way, such as my art teacher and acupuncturist. As time went on, I became more excited and added my former therapist and the members of my group therapy. I didn't really think they would come but two of them did, which was an absolute joy. When I first moved to Oxford, I found life a struggle and engaged a life coach who I spoke with fortnightly. I invited him and although it was sad that he couldn't attend, he sent a delightful letter.

The list was growing including friends of my daughters who I had known for many years and some other art teachers. I then got rather carried away by hiring a female quartet to play during the reception, and a daughter of a friend offered to sing. She was only 13 years old and had a beautiful singing voice. She sang between the main course and the dessert. I ordered small flower arrangements for each table and a cake with yellow decorations, plus a book and artist's brushes made in icing to depict my hobbies of writing and painting.

Of course all my precious immediate family were with me and totally unbeknown to me, Sarah and Jules has contacted everyone who had been invited and asked them to send a photo and a message, which Sarah put in two large, beautiful albums which somehow came over as hand luggage from California. Sarah's husband Shawn told me he hadn't seen the top of their dining room table for weeks!

After tea and cutting the cake, guests slowly began to leave. A few were staying in local hotels but most meandered home. Some had quite long journeys. My immediate family returned to my cottage where after a while I cut a birthday cake made by two of my granddaughters – Ellen and Annabel.

What a wonderous day it was.

* * *

That same year, my beloved Aunt Kath died at the age of 100. She gradually deteriorated having had good health well into old age. She was living in a residential home in Kent when she died. She had been unhappy there to start with. I was living in Oxford, and she was sad that I'd left Kent, so I went to see her every six weeks. They were precious times. I went to America, not realizing how frail she was, and when I got home her daughter told me that she had died. I was devastated. She had been such a special lady in my life – a great character – and, of course, a great disciplinarian. But there was also a light-heartedness about her which was a joy to be near. She had a childlike enthusiasm for life.

My relationship with Aunt Kath was of paramount importance to me. She was totally honest and trustworthy. One of those unique people who never gossiped. It never crossed her mind to do so, which was unheard of in my family where everyone seemed to know everything about everyone. I felt she always had my back. I never thought anyone else did.

When I told Aunt Kath about the abuse, she listened to me, but I know she didn't understand what I was saying. Or if she did, she chose not to. And quite honestly, if I hadn't done the work that I have and someone told me a similar story, I'm not sure that I would have understood either.

CHAPTER TWENTY-ONE

In February of 2020, while working on my memoirs, I read for the first time a tiny diary my mother kept when she was aged just 10. The year was 1918, and she was in hospital having her tonsils removed. The first page reads: "Breakfast at 5.30, then knitting and reading, I got washed and did my hair, cleaned my teeth and nails. Went for a short walk, more reading until 10.15 then operation."

I don't know why I felt so moved reading it, but I was. To think my dear crazy chaotic, organising, creative, loving fun sad, alcoholic mother was once a little girl in hospital about to have an operation is so poignant.

Next day: "Can't talk much today because my throat is so sore. I'm going to have a bath this evening."

Next day, "Please don't talk too much, mother."

A few days later: "I had some calves foot jelly

yesterday. Had bread and milk for breakfast this morning but couldn't eat much. I have written to Don this morning."

This was the most moving comment as Don was her first cousin – a few years older – and destined to become my father. Yes, they married when my mother was 23 years old, much to the concern of many, on both sides of the family. I think I realised, reading this for the first time, that they were destined to be together in this lifetime.

My parents were actually first cousins. This didn't go down well with my maternal grandmother who asked, "What will your aunts say?" But what family members had to say about it were the least of my parents' worries. We know today that cousins marrying and having children together can unleash a slew of genetic problems. But this wasn't so widely known in the 20th century. When Bill was ill and then died, I absorbed from various adult conversations that people believed this was due to my parents being cousins. My mother had rhesus negative blood and my father was rhesus positive, which meant my brother likely had rhesus disease. These days this can be treated.

My sister died of breast cancer at 41. Was this as a result of my parents having been cousins? Possibly, but I think it's more likely due to the stress of her broken marriage.

My health has been affected too since I've got a

blood condition called Bernard-Soulier Syndrome. This was diagnosed when I was 42. It's a clotting disorder and the diagnosis explained why I'd always had such heavy periods and haemorrhaged after surgery. Fortunately, it hadn't affected my pregnancies or childbirth as pregnancy hormones curb its impact.

Over the years when my family mentioned the impact of my parents' marriage on the health of their children, I argued against them. I didn't want it to be true. I don't know why it upset me so much, but I suppose it felt as if people were casting aspersions on my parents' relationship. My parents loved each other because they understood each other. They understood each other's families and sense of humour. They didn't have the confidence to look outside that world.

At the local cemetery, my mother had bought a plot for four next to her mother and father-in-law. Sweet young Bill was first to be buried, then my father, then mother and then I organized for Shirl's ashes to go in there. I went to see Bill, Dad and Mum many times over the years, then when I was towards the end of my therapy, I had a realization and went and told them, "I'm not coming anymore, I've moved on."

Looking back over everything that has befallen my family, I can see that's just the way it was and the way it was meant to be. I'm just so pleased I've been alive long enough to develop new awareness and do it differently. I had a second chance and not many people have that. I don't always succeed but I'm doing it differently now. It's a great treat that I've had that second chance. One of my greatest achievements has been to learn that is okay to show emotions. And I am no longer the Rock of Gibraltar. I assume that other people know how to sort things out themselves.

I think if I had my time again, I wouldn't do anything differently. I do believe that everything has happened as it has meant to. The girls tell me I have stayed alive for a long time because I'm meant to, because I'm brave enough and wise enough to face everything.

The family dynamic? I've stopped that in all its tracks. It's no coincidence that my brother died and another cousin, both Marriott young men, died. They weren't meant to survive in this lifetime. Only Graham's son Billy and David's son Douglas have survived. We've just drawn a line under it and have said, "No more now. We're going to do it differently."

My hope for the years to come is love. Unconditional love, compassion and tolerance. I hope that we can respect each other and have strong personal boundaries but also to feel free to share our true feelings.

It is essential to have a healthy sense of self and

self care. After all, how can we truly love anyone until we know how to love ourselves?

ABOUT THE AUTHOR

Jean Swales was born in Brockley, southeast London, and is very proud of *nearly* being a Cockney, as Brockley is almost within the sounds of the Bow Bells.

She trained as a state registered nurse in Bromley in the 1950s and obtained a diploma in psychotherapy when she *was* in her 50s.

Her previous book was called *Blossom and Me*, about her journey around England interviewing grandmothers.

She enjoys writing, acrylic painting, being in touch with my family, some next door, and some in USA, thanks to Facetime. Also being in touch with nephews and niece in Australia. She also really enjoys having time to explore her "thoughts".

She lives in a very old cottage in an idyllic part of Oxfordshire in a little hamlet called Poffley End next to her middle daughter. She is visited regularly by pheasants, deer, sheep, muntjacs and many birds.

She has been wondering what I want to write about next and would like to explore possibility of writing about life in the London Docks in the last century.

Printed in Great Britain
by Amazon